Effective Complaining

L[illegible]ce

First published 2001

ISBN 0 11 702822 3

Disclaimer

This book put *you* in control. That is an excellent thing, but it also makes *you* responsible for using it properly. Few washing machine manufacturers will honour their guarantee if you don't follow their 'instructions for use'. In the same way, we are unable to accept liability for any loss arising from mistakes or misunderstandings on your part. So please take time to read this book carefully.

This book is not a definitive statement of the law, although at time of writing (1 September 2001) we believe it to be accurate. We cannot accept liability for changes in the law that take place after the publication date, although every effort will be made to show any such changes on the website.

Contents

About the authors

Rosy Border has a First in French and has worked in publishing, lecturing, journalism (majoring in consumer affairs) and the law. She is a prolific author and adapter who stopped counting after 150 titles. Rosy and her husband, John Rabson, live in Suffolk and have a married son in Tennessee.

Angela Clark graduated from LLM at Cambridge University, having already obtained a First Class Honours Degree in Law with Economics. She is currently lecturing in law at Anglia Polytechnic University, where she specialises in Consumer and Commercial Law on the LLB Degree as well as teaching various subjects on the LLM. She has previously worked on a revision of the BPP Business Basics textbook on Law.

Welcome

Welcome to the *You Need This Book First* series. Let's face it – the law is a maze. You cannot hope to find your way through it without a map. This book is your map through the parts of the maze that deal with getting your rights as a consumer. It contains everything lawyers would tell you about the subject, if only they had time (and you had the money to pay them).

Acknowledgements

A glance at the *Useful Contacts* section will show how many individuals and organisations we consulted while compiling this book. Thank you, everyone – especially John Rabson, Chartered Engineer, for his IT support, research and refreshments.

Introduction

What this book can do for you

This book contains advice on:

- your legal rights as a consumer
- complaining about unsatisfactory goods and services including:
  - who to complain to
  - how to go about it
  - what result you can expect
- the buzzwords which are important in this section of the law and what they mean
- answers to some of the most frequently asked questions on the subject
- some sample letters which have got results in the past.

What this book can't do for you

- Be a textbook. Its job is to help you to complain, not to teach you the ins and outs of consumer law. We aim to be streetwise rather than academic.
- Guarantee you will get what you want.
- Replace specific advice you may need on your individual case.

This book empowers you. Think of yourself as a driver using a road map. The map tells you the route, but it is up to you to drive carefully.

So read this book with care. Take the time to do so – do not skip anything. You might even find it quite entertaining at times.

- Everything is there for a purpose.
- If anything were unimportant, we would have left it out.

We have left wide margins for you to make notes.

Hazard signs

As with any legal matter, your own common sense will often tell you when you are on unfamiliar territory and need expert help. But we also alert you to common traps for the unwary. Some situations may arise which are outside the scope of this book, and we alert you to those as well.

Watch out for the hazard sign.

Legal lore

Sometimes we pause to explain something: the origin of a word, perhaps, or why a particular piece of legislation was passed. You do not need to know these things to make use of this book, but we hope you find them interesting.

Power points

Sometimes we pause to empower you to do something. Watch out for the symbol.

Check out our website

Buying this book gives you the right to use our special readers' website.

www.youneedthisfirst.co.uk

Clear English or lawspeak?

Wherever possible, we use WYSIWYG words – *w*hat *y*ou *s*ee *i*s *w*hat *y*ou *g*et – in this book; but there are times when we have either to use legal terms or to use ordinary-seeming words in ways which a non-lawyer may find confusing.

Legal documents have traditionally been written in archaic language, because this wording has stood the test of time – often several centuries – and has been hallowed by the courts. What is more, the use of technical language can sometimes enable specialists to express esoteric concepts in a kind of professional shorthand – let's call it lawspeak – which is useful to them but meaningless to others. This idea of a private language is not new, as anyone who has eavesdropped on a group of professionals – plumbers, doctors, accountants, motor mechanics – can tell you; but lawspeak is more arcane than most. Many lawspeak expressions come from either classical or mediaeval

Latin. Instead of saying something is trivial, a lawyer might say dismissively, *de minimis*. This is short for *de minimis non curat lex*: the law does not concern itself with trifles, or 'Don't let's split hairs'

The same lawyer might lapse into mediaeval French to speak of an unborn child as *en ventre sa mère*. Lord Woolf is trying hard to get rid of Latin/Old French terms, but sometimes they resist translation and lawyers still use them among themselves.

The problem with lawspeak is not so much the Latin and French, however, as its use of English terms which mean different things to lawyers and to non-lawyers – with all the potential for misunderstanding which that entails. We do our best to stick to plain English; and when we don't we explain.

Buzzwords

ABTA – Association of British Travel Agents. This is probably the best-known trade association. Members have to abide by a code of conduct and there is an arbitration scheme (see below) to help you settle disputes.

arbitration – this is an alternative to going to court to resolve a dispute. An independent third party will make a legally binding decision instead.

ATOL – Air Travel Organiser's Licensing – a scheme set up by the Civil Aviation Authority to prevent holidaymakers being stranded if their tour operators or airlines went bust.

claim form – what used to be called a summons; an official court form used in debt recovery and compensation claims. The person making the claim is called a *claimant*; the 'other side' is called the *defendant*.

compensation – payment in money to compensate for loss or damage.

consumer – essentially a customer buying goods or services of a type ordinarily supplied for private use or consumption.

A business customer (including a limited company) may, for some purposes, be a consumer; for example if buying goods which it would not ordinarily buy for the business. Where a business customer deals *on a supplier's standard terms and conditions*, the law implies certain rights which put them into a position equivalent to that of a consumer.

The difficulty with any all-purpose definition of the term *consumer* is that different pieces of legislation use different definitions. The significance of the term *consumer* is that the law protects consumers to a greater extent than non-consumers. A rough rule of thumb is that if you are reading this book as a private individual you are probably a consumer.

contract – a legally binding agreement between two or more parties (see page 29).

damages – the sum of money awarded by the court as compensation.

distance selling – a sales transaction, undertaken in the context of an organised scheme, where the supplier and the customer are not physically in the same place. Examples of distance selling are mail order, tele-sales and e-commerce transactions.

estimate – a provisional assessment (subject to a reasonable margin of error/adjustment) of the *likely* price for goods or services (contrast with *quotation*, below).

exclusion clause – these are normally found in the small print or sometimes in notices, for example in a car park or dry cleaners. It is an attempt to exclude a person's legal liability eg for supplying goods of poor quality. Many exclusion clauses are invalid when applied to a consumer, and some liabilities cannot be excluded at all, so it is always worth challenging them.

force majeure – unforeseen and unavoidable circumstances outside someone's control, which might make it difficult or impossible to carry out a contract.

goodwill gesture/payment – something, typically a voucher, given to the consumer without admission of fault or liability. There is a good Latin term for this: *ex gratia* – literally, 'from kindness/goodwill'

litigant in person – a party to a court action who presents their case personally to the court.

personal service – the delivery by hand of an important document by leaving it with the recipient (rather than using post, fax, email, etc), because that is what the law requires.

Personal service can be tricky if the defendant is keeping out of the way. To effect personal service you must put the document into the hands of the intended recipient or, if they will not accept it, lay it at their feet. You should also always tell the recipient what the document is, particularly if it is in an envelope. You can always choose to deliver a document by personal service. Although it is sometimes compulsory, personal service is the exception rather than the rule. We will alert you when personal service is required.

quotation or quote – an offer to supply goods or perform a service for a *fixed* price.

rejection – this is a remedy available for a serious breach of contract.

summary judgment – in court proceedings, a quickie judgment, available where the defendant tells the court they will defend, but it is obvious to the court that they have no genuine defence.

term – any provision which is part of a contract. They can be *express* or *implied* (see page 29).

unsolicited goods – goods sent to someone without their asking for them to be sent.

Frequently asked questions

This is a long chapter, but if we were to set out the law behind the various questions and answers it would be even longer – and possibly very dull. Every one of these 'FAQs' is based on a real life situation.

I bought a radio in a sale and when I got it home it didn't work. The shop says they don't do refunds or exchanges on sale goods. Is this legal?

Emphatically not. You have exactly the same rights when you buy goods in a sale as at any other time. Take no notice of signs saying 'No refunds on sale goods', except to report the shop to your local Trading Standards Department. Notices like this are against the law and the TSO can prosecute traders who display them.

My 13-year-old daughter has run up an £800 telephone bill with her Internet habit. The telephone company are sending threatening letters. Am I responsible for this debt?

Probably, but please read on. You don't say whether this is your family phone or whether your daughter has made some private deal of her own. A contract will not usually be binding on children under the age of 18, or on people without the mental capacity to understand what they are taking on. Rosy's Dad called this piece of law 'Fools and Bairns' and most traders are aware of this and refuse to trade with either. Check the contract with the telephone company and see who is responsible for paying the bill. If you find, as I fear you will, that the buck stops with you, make friends with someone sensible in the customer services department (see page 76) and start negotiating. Then discuss with your daughter her plans for repaying you.

–My new shirt was sold to me as pure cotton. It's a nice shirt but I have found a tiny label inside saying 'Polyester and cotton'. Have I any redress?

Yes. The trader was breaking the law. The Sale of Goods Act 1979 states that goods must be *as described* and traders are liable even if they were unaware that the goods differed from their description. You are entitled to a refund, so go and get your money back – but be quick, as the shop is entitled to say you have accepted the goods after you have had them for a reasonable time.

–I took a pair of curtains back to a shop because I had measured the window wrongly and the curtains didn't fit. There isn't another pair in the right size and the shop have offered me a credit note. Is this OK or am I entitled to a refund?

You got the measurements wrong and, unless there is something wrong with the curtains themselves, you are not entitled to a refund. See 'No cause for complaint' on page 73. The credit note is a goodwill gesture (see *Buzzwords*) on the part of the shop. Note, however, that some stores – Marks and Spencer and Tesco, for example – do refunds in those circumstances: it pays to patronise them.

I received a present which turned out to be faulty. What can I do?

Although the law has changed to give some Sale of Goods Act rights to the recipients of gifts, few traders seem to know about this and you could still have problems unless you are on excellent terms with the giver. Either ask them to complain on your behalf, or ask them to give you a proof of purchase together with a short note authorising you to complain. Of course, some stores (such as Marks and Spencer) have a no-quibble exchange policy anyway.

I bought a computer which has turned out to be faulty. The shop won't talk to me unless I show them the receipt, but I have mislaid it. Can I still get my rights?

Legally you have the same rights even if you lose your receipt. It does, however, help if you keep a file for receipts, as they are useful evidence of where and when you bought the goods. The shop may, with a little research, be able to find details of your purchase on their own database – you must know the approximate date you bought the computer, and probably also the name of the assistant who served you. And, unless you paid in cash, you should have a cheque stub or credit card voucher, unless you've lost that too! Good luck.

FAQS —**The shop that sold me a malfunctioning camera is insisting the problem is the manufacturer's fault, not theirs. What does the law say?**

The law says it is up to the retailer to deal with complaints about defective goods. You may well have rights against the manufacturer under their guarantee, but that is as well as, not instead of, your statutory rights against the trader.

FAQS —**Do I have the same rights if I buy at an auction as I would if I went to a shop?**

No. Auctioneers often have exclusion clauses in their terms and conditions to shield them from claims – read any catalogues or notices carefully. And once the hammer has fallen you are committed to buying that item and can't back out of the deal. So check out the lots before the sale and if in doubt, don't buy.

FAQS —**I bought a suitcase by mail order which has a faulty lock. The mail order firm say they will refund my money provided I return the faulty case at my expense. Is this right?**

No. You are not legally obliged to return faulty goods at your own expense. Ask for a reply paid label to return it.

I got carried away at a party plan evening and ordered a whole lot of pottery I don't need and can't afford. What can I do?

Cancel – quickly; you should be OK. There is a code of practice covering both doorstep and party plan selling. If the party plan organisers are members of the Direct Selling Association Limited (details in *Useful Contacts* on page 147) you have a 14 day cooling off period.

I bought a £10 electric iron in a chain store. The thermostat was faulty and I scorched my best shirt. Can I claim for the damage as well as the cost of the iron?

Yes. Call the shop, tell them what happened and arrange to take in both iron and shirt. It would be helpful if you could find out how much your shirt will cost to replace.

I used my new washing machine for the first time, and it has flooded my kitchen. The trader wants to send a repairman out to fix it, but I don't feel happy about it. Can I insist on a replacement here and now or do I have to try a repair first?

Agreeing to a repair would not affect your statutory rights; that is, if you agreed to have the machine fixed and the repair failed, you would still have the right to reject the machine afterwards. But a machine that flooded your kitchen the first time you used it is clearly faulty and in your shoes I'd stick to my guns and insist on a refund. However if you need a working washing machine and you haven't lost confidence in that model of machine you could try asking for a replacement. And while you're about it make sure you claim for any damage the faulty machine did to your kitchen. Why pay an excess on an insurance claim if the trader can claim on his own insurance?

FAQS —**My expensive new cooker has a manufacturer's guarantee which covers both parts and labour for one year. The salesman is trying to get me to buy 'peace of mind' in the form of a three-year extended warranty, but it isn't cheap and I am dithering about it. Advice, please.**

Sales people usually get a handsome commission on such deals, which is of course why they are so keen to sell them. Our conversation with the trader goes like this:

Us: You've just told me how reliable this machine is.

Salesman: Er – yes.

Us: But now you're asking me to pay £100 for insurance in case your machine conks out after 13 months. Why?

Salesman is lost for words.

We usually ask ourselves how likely we would be to need to spend £100 or more on repairs over a three-year period, what retribution we would wreak on the manufacturer if this happened, and whether we'd do better to put the same amount of money in a high-interest savings account.

I took my dress to the cleaners and they have ruined it. When I complained, the shop assistant pointed to a note on the back of the cleaning ticket saying, 'We cannot accept any responsibility for loss or damage, however caused'. Have I any redress?

Yes. Make sure you are not in a tearing hurry, because this might take a little time. Go into the shop, ask to see the manager and point out gently that since 1994 Trading Standards Departments have had the power to consider whether get-outs like these are unfair (believe us, they are!), and also the power to take the trader to court to stop them from using them in future. Then ask for a refund of the cleaning bill plus the full replacement cost of the dress and stand there until you get it. Whenever another customer comes into the shop, apologise prettily for keeping them waiting and explain the reason for the delay. We'll see who caves in first.

My husband ordered a hand-tailored wedding suit from a very expensive tailor for our wedding day. Two days before the wedding he went for his appointment for the final fitting and was told that it would not be finished as they had a large order to fulfil for a shop in London. We were both terribly upset and he had to go out and buy another, off-the-peg suit for our wedding day. Is there anything we can do?

Yes, when your husband instructed the tailor to make his suit they both entered into a contract. One of the terms of their contract was that the suit was to be ready for a certain date, ie your wedding day. Get your husband to ask the tailor for the cost of his off-the-peg suit plus compensation for the inconvenience and upset caused. If this gets you nowhere, you could sue the tailor in the County Court. See page 91.

I contacted a local builder to replace a couple of tiles on my roof. We didn't discuss the cost until he had finished the job, at which point he demanded £150. I was shocked but he got very nasty when I said I couldn't pay that amount. He accepted £50 on account but said he will be back for the rest. Help!

You should report this builder to Trading Standards; he sounds like a cowboy to us. You need only pay a reasonable price, and £150 for a couple of tiles sure as hell ain't reasonable. Get some quotes from other builders and write to your cowboy builder telling him what price you feel is reasonable. If this is more than you have already paid enclose a cheque 'in full and final settlement'. Do not be bullied. Don't be afraid of threats, it is very unlikely he would want to take this to court and if he did you are likely to win. If he turns nasty, talk to the police.

I have just had my central heating serviced and part of the comprehensive service included changing some washers in my radiator taps. Only a week later I noticed some of the system was leaking and I got

the plumber out again to take a look. He says that the washers must have been defective and he replaced them. However, he charged me another call out fee and the leakage has damaged my wallpaper. I am not satisfied – but is there anything I can do?

We're not surprised you are unhappy. We would be extremely cross with your plumber, how dare he charge *you* for *his* problems!

He is strictly liable for the quality of the materials he uses and if the materials – ie the washers – caused the problem, he should refund the extra call out charge plus pay you compensation for any damage. However, it sounds to us as if this was a cover story for his bad workmanship. If he is a member of a trade association you could try reporting him to them. Report him to Trading Standards, as there is a chance they may have received other complaints about him and yours may be the last piece in the jigsaw. And next time use another plumber – preferably one recommended by a friend.

I have recently had several pairs of tights come through the letter box with a card stating that they are £1.99 per pair. I started by paying for them as I thought this would be a better option than paying the return postage and having nothing to show for it. However, they keep coming and I really don't want them. What can I do?

FAQS

Good news, Christmas has come early for you. Since 2000, you can now treat any unsolicited goods as a gift.

Wear them, give them to a friend or throw them away: the choice is yours. If the supplier is demanding payment you should report this to Trading Standards, as demanding payment for unsolicited goods is now a criminal offence (see page 45).

–I have ordered some goods using the Internet but nothing has arrived yet. I'm also worried that my credit card details could be used fraudulently by someone else.

Have you been supplied with a written copy of the details of your contract? (see page 37). If not, you can cancel the order. If you are happy to continue with the transaction, the goods should arrive within 30 days of the order being placed unless you have agreed to different terms. As far as your credit card is concerned, you can cancel any payment made fraudulently by someone not acting on your behalf, and you are entitled to be re-credited by your card issuer. It is up to the card issuer to prove you did authorise the payments, if there is disagreement.

–I was telephoned by a very persistent young man who wanted to sell me a carport. He refused to take no for an answer and became quite rude. In the end I agreed just to shut him up. I know this was stupid and I now regret it – but is it too late?

Hopefully not. You are now entitled to written confirmation of the details of your purchase and you then have a 'seven working days' cooling-off period to change your mind. If you haven't yet received confirmation or you only received it in the last couple of days write a short letter to the supplier cancelling your agreement, and send it *now*!

Our holiday was a disaster, the food was inedible, the accommodation was small and smelly, our flights were delayed and our luggage lost. On top of all this we were sent to a different hotel from the one we were booked into and it had none of the facilities listed in the brochure. All the travel firm will offer is a £200 voucher for another holiday with them. Do I have to accept this?

No. If you are sure of your ground, you can sue them in the Small Claims Court. District judges have recently shown considerable sympathy towards the victims of holiday hassles. See page 91 for details.

I am about to fly for the first time, and have heard horror stories about lost baggage. What do I do if the airline loses my suitcase?

There is nothing quite so disheartening as watching the carousel going round without your case on it. Eventually the carousel is empty and your luggage is still nowhere to be seen. But help is at hand. Before you leave the baggage reclaim area, go to the baggage handling office and ask for a Property Irregularity Report. Insist on a copy of the form, and also a copy of your baggage tag – you would have been given this at check-in. This will help the airline to locate your luggage and return it to you.

If this happens at the start of your holiday, you are entitled to essentials; ask your airline (for flights only) or tour operator (if you are on a package tour) for permission to buy items to tide you over. A change of underclothes and some toiletries would be the absolute minimum. Hang onto the receipts to support your claim.

In the very unlikely event of your case going permanently AWOL, you are entitled only to a basic £14 per kilo (at the time of writing) of checked luggage. This is not going to buy many Versace shirts, which is where your travel insurance will kick in.

Suppose they just damage your case? You can claim compensation, but you must do so within seven days of the damage. Late baggage claims have a 21-day deadline.

If it's any comfort, Rosy has flown at least 100 times and has never, ever had her luggage lost or mislaid. Either such problems are rare or she's been amazingly lucky...

— The Air Transport Users' Council (details in *Useful Contacts* on page 138) advises you to label your baggage – inside and out. We also advise you to mark the case itself so that you can easily spot it on the carousel. We favour those webbing straps with your name and telephone number woven into the fabric, but other people go for stick-on motifs ... whatever grabs you.

I booked my holiday with a tour operator whose travel insurance is very expensive. Do I have to take out their travel insurance, and do I really need to bother with insurance at all?

No, and yes! You are not legally obliged to take out the travel insurance offered to you by your tour operator or travel agent. However, you are strongly advised to take out insurance, as things can and do go wrong. Beware an enticingly cheap deal as it may not offer you the best cover. Shop around, but compare what you are getting and make sure the cover is adequate for *your* needs (eg will it cover you whilst bungee jumping in Australia?).

The Association of British Insurers (details in *Useful Contacts* on page 138) offers a useful leaflet on travel insurance.

I have booked an expensive holiday and now I am worried in case the tour operator or the airline goes out of business. Can I protect myself?

Yes. In fact you have probably done so already, without knowing it. Package holidaymakers who travel by air are protected by the ATOL (Air Travel Organiser's Licensing) scheme, which is organised by the Civil Aviation Authority. ATOL has been going for nearly 30 years. Its mission: to save travellers from losing money or being stranded abroad if their tour operator goes belly up. Always check that your tour operator is ATOL-protected before you book a holiday. Most are. So with any luck you will be able to dig out your receipt and breathe again.

As for flights, scheduled flights can be iffy. You may be covered, you may not. If it is a scheduled flight and you booked through a flight consolidator (someone who sells the flights of several airlines), their ATOL will cover you. Note that if you book direct with an airline, or are sent an airline ticket instead of an ATOL receipt, you will not be covered. But how likely is a big airline to go bust without warning?

The CAA has a website (details in *Useful Contacts* on page 138), which explains travellers' rights and tells you which tour operators have ATOLs, which have recently gone bust and what to do if you think any of this might affect you.

FAQS —**I have booked a holiday for September this year, but am now expecting a baby due that month. Can I transfer my holiday to my friend, or do I have to lose the money I have already paid?**

Under the Package Holidays Regulations (see page 57) whenever a consumer books a package holiday they are entitled to transfer the holiday if they are prevented from taking it themselves. However, you must tell the tour operator as soon as possible to give them reasonable notice. Also be careful who you transfer it to as you remain liable for the balance of the price if they fail to pay!

Think before you buy

In an ideal world, you would never need a book about effective complaining because nothing you bought would ever give you cause for complaint. We do not live in an ideal world, but you can still do a great deal to help yourself by thinking before you buy.

Legal Lore

Most people have heard the Latin tag *Caveat emptor* – literally 'Let the buyer beware'. The full version, which rather fewer people know, is *Caveat emptor, quia ignorare non debuit quod ius alienum emit* -'Let the buyer beware, for he ought not to be ignorant of that which he is buying from someone else'. In other words, 'Think before you buy; make sure you know what you are letting yourself in for'. Much legislation has been passed since then to protect you, the consumer, but you still need to keep your wits about you, otherwise the law will not be able to help.

Here are some points to consider before parting with your money:

- Is what you are buying really what you are looking for?
- Is it (if applicable) the right size, colour, etc for your needs?
- Will you still like it after you have got it home?
- Can you realistically afford it?

- Could you get a better deal elsewhere?
- How are you going to pay: cash? Credit card? Some other form of credit?
- Has the trader got a good reputation – and will the trader be contactable if something goes wrong?
- What (if appropriate) is the after sales service like?

We all make the occasional impulse buy; and we all know of impulse buys which were emphatically a Good Move. Unfortunately, many impulse buys prove to be a Bad Move. So do think it through first.

Right is might

A determined consumer *who is in the right* will usually get a satisfactory outcome quite easily. In our experience the vast majority of complaints have a happy ending. This is because:

- there are laws to compel traders to treat their customers fairly;
- Trading Standards departments (see page 71) are happy to give free advice and, if necessary, lean on traders who do not play fair;
- in general, traders prefer their customers to be satisfied; otherwise they would eventually run out of customers;
- most traders can do without the hassle of a protracted dispute.

It is when the trader's idea of fair treatment does not coincide with yours that you need to start asserting yourself. If, on your first approach, a trader is less than helpful and reasonable, do not give up in disgust: that is what they would like you to do. Repeat your mantra to yourself: *right is might*. If you have a valid complaint, the law is on your side and you have a right to get the matter sorted out in a way which is fair to you both.

How far you will have to go to get your rights depends on many factors, including how obstinate and/or obstructive the trader is. If you have right on your side, and the will to win, win you will. Right is might.

In a few extreme cases, you may need to go to court to get your rights. Have no fear! The Small Claims Court is geared to the needs of the litigant in person (see *Buzzwords*) and if your cause is just, the judge is likely to find in your favour. Besides, the mere threat of court action – an experience which will cost them both time and money – may be just what you need to bring a recalcitrant trader to heel. See page 91 for further advice.

Emotional wear and tear – is it worth it?

It is time to be realistic...Do you loathe arguments? Are you shy or lacking in self-confidence? Does the thought of having a row with someone upset you? Some people dread confrontation so much that they will do almost anything for a quiet life. If you are like that, and if there is a real possibility that the emotional stress of a dispute will harm your health, ask yourself whether, for example, a dispute over £14.99 is worth the stress. Then take heart...

We are naturally fairly confident and actually find a little mild confrontation quite stimulating. The enemy usually senses this, realises we mean business and capitulates forthwith. Not everyone is like us – *but with some basic legal lore and the sample letters and other guidelines in this book you can, if you wish, pretend to be like us and get the same results.*

How busy are you, and how much is your time worth? It is tempting to say the principle is what matters, but if winning a £50 argument costs you £100 in lost working time you have lost out. Be objective about this. If necessary, settle for less than you are entitled to. Alternatively, if a lot of money is involved, consider paying for professional assistance rather than doing it all yourself.

The consumer and the law

There is a lot of legislation to protect the consumer. Only a lawyer, a Trading Standards Officer – more about these splendid people on page 71 – or indeed a trader determined to weasel out of their obligations, will need to master all the legislation in detail. Nobody expects an ordinary consumer to do so, but in all circumstances where goods are bought and sold and money changes hands your mantra should be *Sale of Goods Act 1979*. This Act governs all transactions where goods are bought and sold for a price, and it is now backed up by European law.

There are some situations in which a consumer is not covered by the Sale of Goods Act. The buzzword here is 'price' – for a deal to be covered by the Act, money has to change hands. The Sale of Goods Act does not, for example, cover situations in which you merely swap or exchange goods. Those circumstances would come under a different piece of legislation (more about that anon). However, if a transaction combines swapping or exchanging with actual money (such as swapping your old cooker for a new model with a cash adjustment), the money element means that the deal would usually be covered by the Sale of Goods Act 1979.

If your problem does not involve a sale or even goods, don't despair. Other contracts such as hire (hiring unsafe or faulty DIY products, for example) or contracts for services (dry cleaning or a car service) are covered by another Act, the Supply of Goods and Services Act 1982. This contains equivalent protection – see page 64.

A binding contract

Most people have come across contracts in the course of their employment; but there are many kinds of contract. Buying and selling is a contract between you and the seller. Every contract is governed by 'express' and 'implied' terms. In the case of consumer transactions, the *express* terms of the contract are there for all to see. They are the terms agreed by the buyer and seller about that particular transaction either in writing or orally in the conversation between the parties.

Here's how it works. Bert is a shopkeeper. In his shop are some T-shirts at £5 each. You choose one, check it is the right size and hand over £5. Bert takes your money, puts the shirt in a bag and gives you a receipt. You thank him and walk off, well pleased. The *express* terms of the contract in this case are minimal – just the price we have agreed for the item.

However, there are other terms which are *implied* – you and Bert have not discussed them, and if all goes well you may never need to – but because of the 1979 Act those terms are *implied* in your transaction (not stated, but there nevertheless). Like the works inside a radio, they are there for a purpose and, although if all goes well we seldom need to examine them, we all know they are there. Bert cannot wriggle out of those implied terms in a contract with a consumer, because he has a statutory duty – one which is imposed by law – to abide by them. And if he fails in that statutory duty you will have a valid cause for complaint.

Supply of goods

You have a legal right to expect:

1. Safety

The goods you buy must be *safe* for their intended users. *It is a criminal offence to supply unsafe goods*.

This in general applies to second-hand products as well as to new ones. Antiques, and newer items which clearly need repair, renovation or some degree of 'doing up', would be exempt, provided you were told clearly at the time that the item needed attention. So, to sum up:

- the *new* microwave oven Bert sells you must not catch fire;
- nor must the *second-hand* one Bert sells you as being in good working order; but
- the *second-hand* microwave he offers you, *clearly labelled 'Not working' or 'Needs attention'*, would not be covered.

As well as general guidelines about product safety, there are also product directives for specific classes of goods such as toys. The law says that customers must be provided with appropriate safety warnings.

And, if that dodgy microwave injures you, Bert is liable even if he is not the manufacturer of the goods, for example if he is just the distributor or retailer, if he knows that the microwave is dangerous.

For further guidance see the DTI leaflet entitled *The General Product Safety Regulations 1994, Guidance for Businesses, Consumers and Enforcement Authorities.*

2. Quality

The goods must be of 'satisfactory quality'. In brief this means that the goods must be durable (unless, of course, they are by nature perishable: no one expects a kipper to be durable), safe and free from defects – even minor ones.

Goods must meet the standard that a reasonable person would regard as acceptable, bearing in mind

- the way the goods were described;
- their price;
- any other relevant circumstances.

The fact that the seller (let's suppose it is still Bert) is blameless, is no defence to the customer's legal rights and remedies. If, however, he tells a customer about a defect before purchase and the customer buys in true knowledge of the defect, then Bert will not be responsible – unless the defect makes the goods unsafe – see above. A good example is the sweater marked down to half price, with a coloured sticker showing the small snag that is the reason for the reduction.

3. Fitness for their purpose

The Act says that the goods must be reasonably fit for their purpose. So if a trader sells waterproof watches, they must keep out the water.

To be sure of your ground in this respect, it is sensible for you, the customer, to tell the trader that you plan to use the goods for a particular purpose ('I do a lot of scuba diving and I need a watch that will work underwater'). If you have done so, your new watch must be fit for that purpose – unless of course the trader warns you that it won't do, but you persist in buying it anyway, in which case you deserve all the hassle you will undoubtedly get. So a customer who tells a trader that they will be using the watch for deep sea diving has the right to expect it to carry on working at great depths.

4. Price

It is a criminal offence to make misleading price claims about goods or services. A good example is the advertisement saying 'Was £299, now £199'. To comply with the law, that item must previously have been offered for sale at £299. You will sometimes see in very small print in mail order catalogues notes like 'Offered at this price in July 1999'. That keeps it legal, even if the 1999 price was a blatant try-on and nobody bought! It is, however, legal for retailers to say 'RRP [recommended retail price] £299, our price £199' as long as it is the price actually recommended by their manufacturer or supplier and is not out of line with actual prices when it is first used.

If you come across a price indication that you think is misleading, contact your local Trading Standards Department (see page 71) and ask them to look into it.

5. Description

Any description of the goods must be accurate. Giving a false description is a criminal offence. This includes descriptions in advertisements as well as descriptions on packaging and oral descriptions. The seller will be committing the offence even if they make the false description unintentionally (as in the case of the polycotton shirt in FAQs on page 10). Furthermore, one of the implied terms of the seller's contract with your customer is that the goods correspond with the description of them.

This, like every part of the Act, applies to goods bought in sales – but if something is labelled 'seconds' or (as you sometimes find in food shops) 'grade II' you cannot expect them to be perfect.

6. Weights and measures, etc

The Grocer trembles; for his time,
Just like his weight, is short.

(G K Chesterton, *The Song against Grocers*)

Trading Standards departments used to be known as Weights and Measures departments. Their role has broadened considerably in recent years, but they still check traders' scales and other measures for accuracy.

Where appropriate, goods must be supplied by reference to an accurate statement of their weight (eg 250 grams), measure (eg 1 metre) or volume (eg 1 litre). Certain goods must be sold in quantities made known to the customer at or before the time of sale.

Some goods have, by law, to be sold in metric weights and measures and traders can be prosecuted for failing to do this. They say, quite rightly, that a lot of people still find metric weights and measures confusing. To get over this problem, many traders show their prices in both metric and imperial. Our local butcher advertises his mince at £1.25 for 454 grams and we all know where we are.

In some trades weights and measures are still in a transitional stage. For example, many DIY shops sell their goods in a bewildering blend of metric and imperial measures.

7. The right to sell

The seller must have the right to sell the goods (so they must belong to the seller, or the seller must have the owner's authority to sell them).

Additionally, traders may need a licence before they have the right to sell certain goods (examples are alcohol, medicines and firearms). And there is a range of goods which the law does not allow anyone to sell to under-age customers. Examples are knives, fireworks, tobacco and alcohol. Young people may need to prove they are old enough before a trader will do business with them.

8. Conformity with any sample

The law says that the goods the trader sells you must be the same as any sample you show – and this means *strictly* the same as the sample. For instance, you buy floor tiles on the strength of a sample tile in the shop. The tiles the trader later supplies, through no fault of their own, are subtly different. You have the right to reject the goods unless, before you buy, the trader has made clear that the goods may vary, and the margin of variation. An example of this is the Oriental rug which, because it is handmade, may differ slightly in size and colouring from the samples on show. Responsible traders make this clear.

The right to check

Along with all this comes the right to examine goods before accepting them. If the goods are faulty, or do not in some other way comply with the contract terms, the consumer has the right to return them and obtain a refund. Note that the trader cannot get round these obligations by getting the customer to sign a delivery note saying they accept the goods.

If something arrives on the doorstep and the delivery man is anxious for a signature, always put 'Unexamined' beside your signature.

This right to examine is of course important with mail order transactions, where your choice is guided by the picture in the catalogue. Print quality varies and the mauve trousers you chose from the picture may turn out to be dayglo pink. You have the right to return them and get a refund. To be fair, reputable mail order firms make this very easy by offering reply paid labels for 'returns'. It pays to patronise firms like this.

Mail order and other 'distance selling'

When you contract to purchase goods or services (other than financial services)

- over the telephone,
- by mail, eg catalogue home shopping, or
- over the Internet,

you are now protected by a special set of rules, the Distance Selling Regulations 2000. They would also protect you if you made use of the new opportunities to purchase over your mobile telephone or via digital television.

The bad news is that these rules will only cover purchases which are made *exclusively at a distance*. So, for example, they would not cover you when a telephone call is followed up by a home visit (eg certain double glazing firms), as the contract will actually be made face-to-face.

But *the good news* is that you still have important rights in that situation – including an opportunity to change your mind and cancel the contract (see FAQs on page 18).

So what rights have you got when you buy by 'distance selling'? Here they are.

The right to information before you buy

The law says that before you enter into a distance contract for most goods and services, the supplier must provide you with certain information in a clear and understandable manner, such as:

- Who is the supplier, and, if payment in advance is required, what is his address? (This is important as it will help you get a refund if things go wrong.)
- A description of the goods or services you are buying.
- The price including VAT, and the period for which the offer or price is valid, together with any delivery charges.
- Arrangements for payment, delivery or performance.

- Whether substitutes will be provided if goods or services are unavailable, and whether the cost of returning substitutes is borne by the supplier.
- Any minimum period for permanent or recurring supply, eg if you contracted by telephone to have your windows regularly cleaned.
- Your cancellation rights.

Many websites are currently failing to honour their obligations to tell consumers they have a right to cancel – so it is worth remembering that you have this right. If you know a supplier who is not providing this information, you should tell your local Trading Standards Department.

No flannelling!

How often have you sat down with a TV dinner to watch *The Bill* only to have the telephone ring and be pestered by tele-sales callers. The Distance Selling Regulations now state that telephone callers trying to sell must state who they are and what their purpose is at the *beginning* of the call. None of this 'We're conducting a survey...' nonsense. This will give you the choice of listening to their offer or going back to watch *The Bill* in peace.

The right to written information

Again, for most goods and services you are entitled to confirmation of most of the above in writing, ie by post, fax or 'another durable medium' such as e-mail. The most important right here is the right to written information about your *right to cancel* and how it may be exercised. In particular you must be told if you need to return goods to the supplier and, if so, who has to bear the costs of return. If the contract is for more than a year or for an unspecified duration, you also need to be told of any conditions attached to cancellation.

You must also be given the address of the supplier in writing, to which you can address any *complaints*, and information about guarantees and after-sales service. This information needs to be given to you either before you enter the contract *or*, at the latest, by the time the goods are delivered or the service is being performed.

Where the contract is for a service, other than one performed at a distance (eg by mail or over the Internet), the consumer needs to be informed that they cannot cancel once performance of the service has started, eg once the workmen have started installing your double glazing.

The right to cancel

When?

Where the supplier of *goods* provides you with the written information mentioned above, you have seven working days after the goods are delivered. However, if they fail to provide you with the written information required prior to delivery, they are allowed to do so within three months of supplying the goods, in which case you have until seven working days after you receive the information to cancel. If the supplier does not even do this, you have until three months and seven working days after you receive the goods to cancel!

Example: You order goods on 31 May by telephone. You are supplied with the goods on 23 June. You do not receive any written notice of your right to cancel, etc, until 31 August, when the company's lawyer tells them to start complying with the rules! You have from 31 May until 10 September to cancel. That should give you plenty of time to think it over...

Services by distance selling

Where you contract to purchase *a service* the rules are slightly different. Were you provided with the written information by the date the contract was concluded? If so, you have seven working days after the contract was made in which to cancel. Where the information is provided within the three months following the contract date (*not* the carrying out of the service), you have seven working days after you receive the information to cancel. Where the information is not provided before the contract date or within the following three months, you have three months and seven working days after the contract date to cancel!

However, remember that unless your supplier has agreed differently, you will not be able to cancel once the supplier has started carrying out the service, provided you were informed about this.

How do you cancel?

You should put your intention to cancel in writing and date it. You should address it to the supplier (or anyone else they have previously told you is a person to whom notice of cancellation should be given). You should then take or send it to the supplier's (or other named person's) last known address. The date of posting will be accepted as date of cancellation.

Alternatively, notices of cancellation can be faxed or sent by e-mail to the last known business fax number or e-mail address. Notices served on a limited company may also be sent to the address of its secretary or clerk, and notices to partnerships may be sent to a partner.

Note that there are important exceptions where you *cannot* cancel. The most relevant of these are personalised goods or goods made to the customer's specification (how could the trader possibly find another buyer for that purple bathrobe with your name on?); audio or video recordings or computer software which has been unsealed by you; newspapers and magazines; and betting or lottery services. (And, need we say, flowers – imagine what a bunch of freesias would look like after you had examined them in your home for seven days.)

Getting your money back

If you cancel a distance contract within the cancellation period, you are entitled to a *full refund* and the return of any property supplied as security. However, if the contract states that you must return goods upon cancellation, and you have not done so; or you did but at the supplier's expense, the supplier may make a charge up to the cost of recovering the goods. The supplier has up to *30* days from cancellation to refund your money. This is of course if there is nothing wrong with the goods. If they are faulty, you would be entitled to a reply paid label.

The notice of cancellation will also have the effect of cancelling any related credit agreements. However, any credit will need to be repaid (unfortunately!) and the agreement remains enforceable in relation to the credit and interest. But if you repay the amount of the credit within a month of cancellation (or before your first instalment is due if the credit is repayable this way), you will not incur any interest charges.

If you have given goods in *part-exchange*, what happens to them upon cancellation? The supplier has ten days from cancellation to return the goods to you in substantially the same condition as when you handed them over. Failing this, the supplier must pay you a sum equal to the part-exchange allowance.

Returning goods

Before you cancel, you must have retained the goods and taken reasonable care of them. When you cancel you are under a legal duty to restore them to the supplier *if requested*, and to take reasonable care of them until then.

Note, however, that you have no duty to return the goods unless they ask you – and refund your postal etc expenses. Otherwise you do not have to take the goods anywhere. You only need to hand over the goods at your own premises and upon a written request, which they must make within 21 days of cancellation. After that, your duty to take care of the goods ends – the law recognises that you can't be expected to take care of them forever.

However, some contracts say specifically that you must return the goods upon cancellation. In this case the supplier has six months from cancellation in which to ask you to return the goods. They can also make you do this at your own expense, provided you were informed in writing of this condition.

If you unreasonably refuse to return goods upon request – in other words, if they ask you to return them and you say 'Shan't!' – your duty to retain the goods and look after them continues. You may also find yourself being sued – so it's better if you just hand them over!

Going ahead with the contract

Unless you agree differently, the supplier must carry out their side of the deal within *30 days* of your sending your order. If they cannot perform on time they must tell you this; and they have a further *30 days* to refund any money you have paid *unless*

- the contract provided for them to supply a substitute, and
- a substitute of equivalent quality and price is available.

Note that in the case of goods and services linked with outdoor leisure events such as the Grand National, which cannot be rescheduled (would anyone dare try it?), the consumer and supplier can agree that no refund will be made. So beware – and check those terms carefully.

For further information on your rights when purchasing by mail order contact the OFT (Office of Fair Trading – details in *Useful Contacts* on page 151) and ask for their leaflet *Shopping from Home: The Facts at your Fingertips*.

And finally, a word about unsolicited goods

Ever had goods drop onto your doormat that you don't remember ordering? Have you felt pressured into paying for them? *Any goods which are unsolicited, in other words goods which you have not asked for, are yours to keep as a gift.* You do not have to pay for them, and in fact requesting payment is a criminal offence on the part of the supplier. There are a few conditions, so make sure these apply:

- They were sent to *you* for you to acquire (if *your* address is on the package, that is proof enough).

- You have no reasonable cause to believe they were sent for business rather than personal use (take the example of the tights in the FAQs on page 17).
- You have not agreed to acquire or return them (in other words you have not ordered them or entered into any agreement about them).

So if, for example, you receive a package with the wrong name and address, this may not be unsolicited, as it was not meant for you. Similarly, if you receive something which is commercial or industrial in nature, it was probably sent for business purposes and is not unsolicited. Our advice in this situation is to keep the goods safe and let the sender know you have them. Ask for a prepaid address label to return them. You do not want to be sued for the price of an unwanted box of printer cartridges!

—Note that it is now a criminal offence to demand payment for unsolicited *services*. So, if you receive an e-mail requesting payment for a service you didn't ask for, report the matter to Trading Standards.

Special rules for food and drink

He sells us sands of Araby
As sugar for cash down;
He sweeps his shop and sells the dust,
The purest salt in town,
He crams with tins of poisoned meat
The subjects of the King,

And when they die by thousands
Why, he laughs like anything.
(G K Chesterton's *Grocer again*)

Not any more he doesn't! The food safety legislation aims to 'control all aspects of food safety from the plough to the plate'. The law gives customers the right to expect that:

- The product is fit for human consumption. It is a criminal offence to sell, or even advertise for sale, food or drink which does not comply with food safety requirements. And under the legislation, food can be unfit for human consumption even if there is no health hazard. For example, it is illegal to sell foods after their 'Use by' date even if the food is obviously quite sound. That is why you see assistants wheeling trolleys full of appetising-looking food which they have removed from display. You'd love to buy it cheaply, and it would probably be quite safe to eat, but they would be breaking the law if they sold it to you because it is past its sell-by date. Yes, it's a wicked waste, but it's the law. The legislation is wide-ranging and detailed. The Food Safety Department or Environmental Health Team (their titles vary, but their job is the same) of your local authority can advise.
- The nature, substance and quality of the product supplied are consistent with what the customer asked for. So, if the customer asks for diet lemonade, supplying ordinary lemonade will be a criminal offence (unless, of course, the customer agrees to vary their order).

- The label gives an accurate description of the product. It is a criminal offence to use a label which gives a false description or is likely to mislead (even if nobody is actually misled!). For example, a strawberry yogurt can't show a picture of a strawberry on the pot unless it comes mainly from strawberries. Mind you, there is as yet nothing to stop producers of battery eggs labelling them 'Fresh Farm Eggs' with a picture of an idyllic country landscape and not a battery shed in sight.
- If the food you offer for sale contains genetically modified (GM) products, it must say so on the label.

You can get further information from the Foodsense series, produced by Department for the Environment, Farming and Rural Affairs (DEFRA). Call 0645 556000 for free copies. You might start with *Preventing Food Fraud* (ref no PB2533), *Food Safety* (ref no PB0551) and *Understanding Food Labels* (ref no PB0553). Full details in *Useful Contacts* on page 135.

Buying cars

After your home, your car is probably your second most expensive purchase. Many people feel passionate about their cars, and take it personally when things go wrong.

Second-hand cars

Your rights in this situation depend on whether you are buying from a dealer or a private seller. If you are buying from a dealer you have some redress if things go wrong – please read on.

If the car you have bought from a dealer is faulty, then you have the rights that the Sale of Goods Act 1979 (see page 27) gives to all consumers. This means that you have the right to a refund from your dealer if the car is not reasonably fit for its purpose or of satisfactory quality. Remember this includes 'durability', so your car must 'go as a car' for a reasonable period of time – and of course *it must be safe*.

The dealer may offer you a repair. The good news is that you now have a real choice. You can accept the repair without affecting your right to a refund if a repair does not solve the problem. So you might wish to go with this choice if you don't want the hassle of having to get another car.

—Make sure they lend you a courtesy car while they are fixing yours.

However, you should also remember that you must exercise your right to a refund relatively quickly. This has caused problems in the past, as consumers haven't found out about their car's faults until it was too late to reject their car and get their money back. Having said that, even then you still have the right to compensation to enable you to have the car put into the condition it should have been in, in the first place. So get back to the dealer and complain.

—You *do not* have these rights against a private seller or – generally – against an auctioneer if the car was bought at auction, so beware: *Caveat emptor* (see page 23) really does apply here!

Description

Whether you buy from a dealer or from a private seller, you do have the right to a *refund* if the car was misdescribed. This is why many second-hand cars have a 'sold as seen' notice on them. However, there may still have been some description attached to them which will entitle you to your money back.

So if, for example, you were unlucky enough to buy a 'cut and shut' (parts of two or more cars welded together), then you might be able to argue a breach of the implied term as to description if only half of the car were a '1997 Ford Mondeo' as described in the newspaper advertisement.

The courts have also allowed the consumer to have a remedy where the car was so defective that it no longer amounted to a car: the consumer had paid for a car and been given a heap of scrap!

If the seller is a dealer, then they may also be criminally liable under the Trade Descriptions Act 1968 if they misdescribe a car or sell a car which has had a false description applied to it. The most common complaint here is that the car has been 'clocked', that is, its odometer has been turned back so that it looks as if it has done fewer miles than in fact it has. The dealer is liable whether he clocked the car himself or is selling a car clocked by someone else – unless he can show he exercised all reasonable care.

If a car has been clocked, it is going to be worth less than you thought, so look out for these warning signs:

- the numbers are out of line;
- the mileage does not correspond with previous MOT certificates or the service schedule;
- the car looks more worn than usual for the miles on the odometer.

Stolen cars

When you buy a car there is an implied term, as with other goods, that the person selling it has the right to sell it. This means that if you buy a car which turns out to be stolen you have a right (in theory!) to compensation from the person who sold it to you. The problem is usually finding that person, as a crook is not going to wait around for you to sue them.

If you do buy a stolen car, then you cannot keep it even though you may have spent thousands of pounds. The person from whom it was stolen is the legal owner and you are only left with your right to sue the seller. If you do not hand it back the legal owner can sue you!

So it is more important for you to avoid buying a stolen car than it is to know your rights after you have bought one. Stolen cars may be 'ringed' or 'cloned' by the thief. Ringed cars are stolen cars with a fresh identity. The thief might buy a car from a scrap yard and then transfer the registration plates to a stolen car of the same make and model, etc. He can then use the registration documents of the scrapped car to sell the stolen one.

Cloned cars are similar, but the thief doesn't actually purchase the car whose identity he is going to use. He uses the number of a car of the same make and model as the one he has stolen and produces or buys fake registration plates for that number. He then forges or buys forged documents. In cloning there is therefore two cars on the road with the same registration number, one legitimate and one stolen.

To avoid buying a stolen car there are some things you can look out for:

- Do the registration plates match the registration document, service schedule and MOT certificate?

- Are there spelling mistakes or alterations on the registration document?
- Is there a watermark on the registration document?
- Does the engine number match the registration document?
- Has the Vehicle Identification Number (VIN) (usually in the engine but check your car's handbook) been interfered with? Does it correspond to the registration document, etc?
- Is there a VIN etched onto the car's windows? Does this match the one on the car? Have areas of glass on the windows or sunroof been scratched off or covered by stickers to avoid you reading the VIN?

Outstanding hire purchase

At one time this was a nightmare for drivers. You buy a lovely car, only to be chased down by a finance company and told that the previous 'owner' never finished paying for it and therefore the finance company were repossessing it. Again, you had the right to pursue the seller for a refund of the price you paid because they didn't have the right to sell; but that was difficult – dodgy sellers would have spent your money before you caught up with them – and an innocent consumer could end up hugely out of pocket.

Today, although the finance company will probably still try to claim the car back, you have a defence – *as long as you bought in good faith*. So do defend your case, don't give away that £6,000 car to the finance company when you don't have to!

And finally, a word about warranties and servicing

Your troubles don't necessarily end when you have bought the car. Cars frequently come with all sorts of warranties. These may be part of the package or may be sold separately. There may be conditions attached to the warranty, for example that the car is only covered if it is regularly serviced by the dealer from whom it is purchased. Unless these conditions are particularly onerous, you ought to comply with them to ensure that your warranty will continue to be enforceable. Remember, however, that any warranty is *in addition* to your rights under the Sale of Goods Act 1979.

If your warranty provider, usually the manufacturer but possibly the dealer, fails to honour his side of the warranty, you may be able to bring a claim for breach of contract. Any onerous conditions may also be challenged as being unfair.

When your car is being serviced you are paying for a service which is covered by the Supply of Goods and Services Act 1982. Thus you have all the rights mentioned in the section on services (see page 64). Most importantly, you have the right to have the service carried out with reasonable care and skill and any parts must be of satisfactory quality. However, if you are in dispute with the garage over this, you should still pay the bill under protest and then pursue your claim in the courts or via a trade association. Otherwise the garage has the right to keep your car until you pay up!

How to deal with your problem

If you feel you are entitled to a refund under the implied terms of your contract (see above – satisfactory quality, fitness for purpose or description), then contact your seller as quickly as possible. If they are uncooperative you may need to go to court to enforce your rights. Put your claim to your seller in writing and keep copies of all correspondence. See *See you in court* on page 91.

If you bought from a dealer who is a member of a trade association you may be able to avoid going to court by using the National Conciliation Service of the Retail Motor Industry Federation, which deals with disputes under the motor industry's code of practice – see *Useful contacts* for details.

If you used credit to buy your car and this was arranged by your dealer, you may also have rights against the credit company under the Consumer Credit Act 1974. This could be especially useful if your dealer has gone out of business.

If you believe you have bought a 'cut and shut', or that your vehicle was clocked or stolen, it is worth contacting your local Trading Standards Department, who can investigate.

For further help

The OFT has pages on its website (see *Useful Contacts* on page 139) called *Buying a used car* and the motoring associations' websites can offer some good advice on what to look for too. Trading Standards also has useful leaflets on this subject.

You could also consider investing in a service such as the RAC Vehicle Status Check or AA Used Car Data Check, which will check to see if the car you want to buy is stolen or subject to outstanding hire purchase and whether the VIN matches the registration number.

The major motoring organisations also provide an inspection service and they will examine the vehicle to see if it is safe, whether there is evidence of a 'cut and shut', etc. You might have to pay for this but you will save a lot more if they find out the car was stolen!

When complaining about a new car which is giving trouble (and we have all come across them in our time), it pays to mount an attack on three targets, preferably simultaneously:

- the manager of the showroom where you bought the car;
- the managing director at company headquarters;
- the managing director at the manufacturers.

Be polite. Be assertive. Be eloquent. Be persistent. Rosy knew she had won when she heard the manager of the showroom say, 'Oh God, it's that lady about the dodgy Fiat. Tell her I'm out and give her anything she wants.'

Holidays from hell

If you have ever had a bad holiday experience you will understand how important it is to have legal regulation in this area. In addition to the Trade Descriptions Act 1968, which can help you if your holiday was knowingly misdescribed, you are now protected by the Package Travel, Package Holidays and Package Tours Regulations 1992.

Note, however, that these regulations only protect you if you have bought a *package* holiday, for example a combination of air travel to Spain and hotel accommodation when you get there. They would not protect you if you booked each of these items separately as an independent traveller.

Before you go: the right to information

The law recognises that you have a right to be given certain information at various stages before you actually go on holiday.

First, before you make a contract you should be provided with information about passport and visa requirements and any health formalities, such as immunisations required. You normally make your contract when you book your holiday.

Secondly, a reasonable time before you depart, you should be provided with the relevant travel information, such as any intermediate stops and connections. You should also be given the contact details of the tour operator's local representative at your destination, or details of some other agency that can help if you have problems.

The party you are contracting with, normally a tour operator, will be *criminally liable* if they fail to provide you with any of this information. If you feel you were not adequately informed, contact your local Trading Standards Officer.

In addition, your travel organiser (normally a travel agent) will be guilty of a criminal offence if they make holiday *brochures* available to you which do not *clearly* indicate the price of your holiday and/or include *adequate* information about the accommodation, meals, etc included. Again, if in doubt complain to Trading Standards.

Were you misled?

The most important provisions in the regulations are designed to prevent you from being misled. The law says that if you are supplied with information about your holiday or its cost which is misleading, the party supplying that information is liable to compensate you for your losses.

Example: your travel agent informs you that a hotel has a swimming pool, fitness suite and air conditioning. That travel agent will be liable to compensate you if the hotel does not have those facilities. The problem with your rights here is proving what was said.

However, the law has a second string to its bow. The regulations make *brochure statements* into implied terms of the contract (see page 29).

This is good news for consumers, as you will now be able to sue the tour operator for compensation for breach of contract if the holiday does not live up to its description in the brochure.

Price

Beware of terms in your holiday contract that allow the tour operator to change the price. If they do wish to do so, find out why. Tour operators can only change the price if their contract allows for prices to be revised both ways, ie they can go down as well as up. Even then the price can *only be changed for certain reasons* – such as a change in transport costs or taxes. This means that a price rise because of an increase in airport taxes or fuel would be allowable, but a change to cover increased hotel costs would not. In any event the price cannot be changed in the month before departure, or for small variations in cost.

Alterations to your holiday

Where the tour operator wishes to make a significant alteration to your holiday, the law again puts implied terms into your contract. These implied terms require the tour operator to notify you as soon as possible about the change, and allow you to withdraw from the contract. You may have three options in this situation:

- obtain a full refund;
- accept a substitute holiday of the same or higher quality, if available;
- accept an inferior substitute, if one is available, together with a refund of the difference in price.

You may also be entitled to compensation.

Cancellation by the tour operator

Again there is an implied term that the consumer is entitled to one of the three remedies listed above and, except in certain circumstances, compensation where appropriate.

Financial security

Rest assured that there is a great deal of regulation in place requiring tour operators to make arrangements to ensure that your money is safe if they become insolvent. There must also be evidence that the operator would be able to get you home again if they became insolvent while you were on holiday. See the FAQ about tour operators that go bust: most package tour passengers are protected by their tour operator's ATOL (Air Travel Organiser's Licence). More details in *Useful Contacts* on page 138.

If disaster strikes!

What do you do if your holiday is a complete disaster? Tour operators are contractually liable for the proper performance of the holiday contract even if some of it was to be performed by other people. In other words, if your hotel is not up to scratch, or you have problems with the airline, the tour operator is also liable. So if your hotel bathroom is flooded or full of cockroaches, your airline loses your luggage or your family fall ill from food poisoning after dining in the hotel restaurant, you are entitled to compensation from your tour operator. This is good news, as trying to sue a Spanish hotel is not going to be easy!

Practically speaking, you need to complain, immediately and forcefully, to the tour rep on site. Take their name and make a note of the date, time and place you complained and what the outcome was, with the rep's comments if you got a dusty answer. Then, if you have not got what you wanted, you need to telephone or fax the head office of the tour operator. If they do not leap into action immediately, warn them that they'll be hearing from you when you get home and collect evidence:

- photographs or videos of grotty accommodation, views of wreckers' yards instead of the promised sea views, etc;
- written comments from fellow holidaymakers.

Then, when you get home, let rip! And be sure to log in on the holiday complaints website (see *Useful Contacts* on page 137) and share your experiences with the world.

And finally, where can you get help?

Holiday consumers are in one way better off than many other consumers. They have a variety of avenues open to them. If complaints to the tour operator don't get you anywhere, you can opt for arbitration or the small claims procedure at the County Court.

ABTA offer an arbitration scheme that is administered independently by the Chartered Institute of Arbitrators (so you should be able to trust them!). If you are shy or are wary of going to court, this might be the better option for you. The procedure is fairly simple and you do not have to attend a hearing. The decision is based on the case that you put in writing, and you are entitled to see the tour operator's defence before it is submitted. However, the compensation you can receive is limited. It has only recently gone up from £1,500 to £5,000 per person, from £7,500 to £15,000 per group. So if you have suffered serious personal injury, for example, or wish to put your case in person, you may wish to go to court. There is also a nine-month time limit for ABTA claims.

It is worth noting that ABTA is, at the time of writing, considering an e-mail resolution service. Details of ABTA are in *Useful Contacts* on page 137.

You may take your case before the County Court under the small claims procedure if your claim is for less than £5,000, or up to £1,000 in personal injury cases. This procedure is much less formal than a normal court hearing and you can represent yourself as a litigant in person (see *Buzzwords*). When the court considers your claim for compensation for a disastrous holiday you may claim an additional sum for loss of enjoyment, not only for yourself but for your family or friends who went with you. More about courts in *See you in court* on page 91. And you might like to use Mr Lucky's claim on page 118 as an example. Don't worry if it seems legalistic; this claim was drafted by a lawyer. Just tell it like it is, in your own words, making sure you include all the important information. Judges are sympathetic towards litigants in person and give them more latitude than they would ever give a professional.

Contracts for services

Has your plumber left you knee-deep in water? Have you received an extortionate demand from your solicitor (!) or has your gasman failed to turn up for three appointments in a row? Do not despair – the Supply of Goods and Services Act 1982 is designed to help you.

First, let us start by repeating the point we made earlier about this Act giving equivalent protection to the Sale of Goods Act 1979. You may recall that the 1979 Act ensures that goods you buy are of a satisfactory quality, fit for their purpose and as described: see pages 33–34. These terms are also implied in contracts for services, where goods are supplied as part of that service. So, if you take your car to be serviced, this means that any new parts supplied by your garage must be of satisfactory quality and fit for their purpose and as described. Again, the supplier of the service cannot wriggle out of these obligations to a consumer.

In addition, however, the 1982 Act also implies other terms that deal with the service element of the contract.

Quality of service

Where a business supplies a service to a consumer, there is an implied term in your contract that the service will be performed with reasonable care and skill. This means that the plumber must be *sufficiently skilled* as a plumber, or that your dentist must demonstrate the standard of care of a reasonable dentist. So, if your plumber forgot to turn the water off before he started work and your kitchen was flooded, you could sue for breach of contract.

Take the example where you employ an electrician to do some wiring and he brings along his apprentice. The apprentice might make mistakes. It is worth remembering that the test is not that the apprentice 'did his best', but to ask what would a *competent, qualified and experienced* electrician have done. You are paying for the organ grinder, not the monkey.

1. It is worth checking to see if a tradesman or firm belongs to a trade association and/or is appropriately qualified before you employ them. A trade association may have a scheme to help you with complaints if things do go wrong. There are several trade associations listed in *Useful Contacts* from page 140 onwards.

2. Never agree to pay for all the work in advance, although you may have to pay some money up front (eg towards materials) before they will start work. Agree to pay the rest when you are satisfied the work is finished and has been carried out properly. Holding even quite a small sum back will give you some leverage if you are not satisfied with the work. If the service supplier incurs further expense putting right his bad workmanship, such as by redoing it, remember that it is his fault and he must pay the extra cost.

3. A firm is responsible for the actions of its employees, so it makes sense to pursue the firm rather than the individual – it is more likely to be insured and be financially able to pay the claim.

Injury or death

A supplier can *never* exclude liability for their negligence if it causes injury or death.

If you contract for a service to be carried out and someone other than yourself is hurt, they may not be able to bring an action in contract, but the supplier should still be liable to them for negligence. For example, if you contract to have a new roof and two days after the work is finished some tiles slip and injure your children or your best friend, they could bring an action against the roofing company for negligence.

(They could also bring an action against you and you, in turn, would need to sue the roofing firm.)

How much will it cost?

You should always agree a price for work before the supplier starts. If a price is given, try to ensure it is a quotation rather than an estimate (see B*uzzwords*). Ask the supplier if the price is fixed (a quote) or a rough guide (an estimate).

Sometimes you may enter into contracts without setting a price and you can be shocked by the final bill. In this situation there is some help. The 1982 Act again implies a term that, where no price has been agreed, a reasonable price will be paid. So, if you think the bill is excessive, it is worth challenging it. Ask around other suppliers to see what they charge and try to negotiate a lower price.

The relevant trade association (see *Useful Contacts* on pages 140 onwards) might also give you an idea of an average price. Offer what you consider reasonable as final settlement of the bill.

If that fails and you still feel strongly enough to resist further payment, things may turn nasty and you may be sued by the supplier and have to argue your case in court. Try to get written quotations from other suppliers as evidence that your supplier's charges were OTT. See *Expert opinions* on page 76.

A note of warning – the 1982 Act will *not* help you if you have previously agreed to an excessive price, only where no price was agreed. Remember *Caveat emptor,* buyer beware! So ask around to make sure you are not agreeing to anything unreasonable.

The only situation where you may be able to get the court to intervene and lower a charge you have agreed to, is where you have entered into credit arrangements and you are being charged a grossly extortionate rate of interest. For more information seek advice on the Consumer Credit Act 1974 from Trading Standards.

When will it be done?

Anyone who has waited in for a repairman who never showed up knows the frustration this can cause. If you have work that needs to be carried out urgently, you should make this clear to the service supplier, preferably in writing. If they agree to a *deadline*, you at least have the comfort of being able to sue them if they fail to meet it, or cancel the contract and go elsewhere.

Legal Lore

When something is time-critical, lawyers say that time is of the essence. You can build the time factor into your contract if you make clear that time is of the essence. So the bridegroom in the FAQs who ordered an expensive suit made time of the essence, because he made it clear that the suit was needed for a certain date, ie his wedding day.

So make time of the essence in your dealings with suppliers. For example, you need your car serviced before driving to Edinburgh for an important business meeting. Inform the garage of the urgency, give them a deadline and make sure they agree. Tell them what will happen if they breach it – you will have to hire another car or catch a train or plane – all expensive options. If, close to your deadline, you discover that they haven't even started on your car and would not be able to finish on time, you will be entitled to cancel your contract and go elsewhere, charging any extra costs to the garage. If you discover they have started but won't be finished by the deadline, ask them to provide an alternative suitable vehicle. If they cannot oblige, work out the cheapest way to get to Edinburgh (should you hire a car, go by train or fly?) and charge the cost to the garage.

Similarly, if you wait in for a service engineer who does not turn up for a set appointment, they will be in breach of contract and you would be entitled to charge them for any consequential losses such as lost pay. Rosy, who always warns people about this before setting a date for the engineer to call, has surprisingly few missed appointments.

There are organisations which voluntarily build into their service contracts some modest compensation to the customer for delays like this. We came across a kitchen firm that offered small goodwill payments if, for example, they were late delivering. This works both ways: they have an incentive to get it right and you get some compensation for your wasted time.

Pulling the plug

If you have not agreed a deadline, when can you say 'Enough is enough'? The 1982 Act is helpful again here. The law says that, where a time is not agreed, a service must be carried out within a *reasonable time*. This will depend on what type of service it is, as some services will obviously take longer than others. You would expect a builder to take longer to construct an extension than knock up a brick wall, for example. If you feel your supplier is taking too long, try to agree a finish date and warn them you may sue if they don't get on with the job. You could also mention that you will complain to Trading Standards about them. A reputable firm may well be spurred on by this.

In praise of Trading Standards

The Trading Standards Department of your local Council is the place to go with any consumer complaint. Goods, services, holidays – they will want to know about them all.

Trading Standards is a good name for what these knowledgeable and dedicated people do: where there is *trading*, they are committed to maintaining acceptable *standards*. To them is delegated the enforcement of a wide range of consumer-oriented legislation, covering areas like product safety, fair trading, weights and measures and environmental controls. They are committed to ensuring honesty and fairness in all business activity and as such they are ready to help both traders and consumers.

Trading Standards Officers (TSOs) are often in the news. Sometimes the publicity is unfriendly. In a high-profile case in 2001 a market trader was prosecuted for contravening EC regulations by selling vegetables in pounds and ounces. He was labelled a 'Metric Martyr' in the press and the TSOs were made to look a bunch of killjoys. Some TSOs are portrayed as champions of public safety, however, as in a case in 2000 in which Trading Standards hunted down and prosecuted a trader whose dangerous toys nearly killed a toddler. They found his source of supply and made a successful prosecution of both trader and supplier.

Somewhere near you – look in your telephone directory – there are TSOs working tirelessly to keep up standards. Most supply large amounts of splendidly readable free leaflets, some home grown, some produced by central government, such as the DTI. My local TSO supplies a free Consumer Action Pack.

If you used your Trading Standards Department to the full, and read all their free literature, you would not need this book: you would have enough knowledge and legal clout to tackle any problem. On the other hand, you'd occupy a lot of their time...

You can find out a great deal more about Trading Standards by visiting their website: www.tradingstandards.net.

No cause for complaint

Before we get down to the business of complaining, let us set out the situations where you have no real cause for complaint (though many traders will give you more than you are legally entitled to, because they would prefer you to be satisfied). You have no cause for complaint if:

- you were warned of any fault before you bought the item;
- you examined the item before you bought it and should have seen the fault;
- you did the damage yourself;
- you made a mistake when you bought the item (see the FAQ about the wrong size curtains on page 10);
- you just changed your mind about the item.

Successful complaining

So far we have discussed your legal rights, with barely a mention of asserting them. The next section of this book deals with complaints technique.

Right, in the form of

- having the law on your side, and
- knowing you have the law on your side,

is a mighty weapon. To be effective, however, your mighty howitzer (or whatever) has to be carefully loaded, cocked, aimed and fired at the right target. That is where strategy comes in.

In other words, there are times when you must point your weapon at the commanding officer, not the poor bloody infantry. First, however, you start at the bottom. Please read on.

Services

First identify the culprit. If you are dealing with an individual tradesman or small firm, try the personal approach first. Most small businesses are keen to keep your goodwill because word soon gets around if they don't. If you are dealing with a large organisation, the various ploys below (see *Go to the top* on page 83) will apply.

Let's suppose first, however, that you are dealing with a local builder rather than British Gas.

Be polite but assertive. See *Be organised*! on page 85 below, and if you need to put something in writing use Standard Letter 3.

You can forestall a great many potential complaints if you make a habit of withholding a small proportion of the bill until you are absolutely satisfied that the work has been completed satisfactorily. If you tell the tradesman at the start of the transaction this will make things clear and – one hopes – encourage them to do a good job.

If they won't play ball

This is when you look in *Useful Contacts* (see pages 140 onwards) for trade associations. We can't generalise, as there are so many, but many trade associations will arbitrate in disputes. They may also be able to put you in touch with someone who can give an expert report on the work in dispute. See *Expert opinions*, below.

How many cowboy builders, roofers, etc belong to a trade association? If you find you are dealing with a cowboy (and it does to some extent serve you right for not using a respectable local tradesman with a reputation to keep up!) you may be better going to Trading Standards or, in extreme cases, the police.

Expert opinions

There are two good reasons for getting an expert opinion to back up a complaint. First, an expert who agrees with you will help you prove your point to the individual. Secondly, if you end up in court the expert opinion will help you prove your point to the judge.

A sensible choice of 'expert' would of course be a reputable practitioner in the same field. Experts' time is valuable and they may not be happy about giving you a report for free. If you do have to pay them, you may be able to claim the cost of their report as well as the cost of putting the problem right.

Before you go to the expense of getting a report, it is worth telling the trader what you plan to do. They may cave in then and there, and save you the expense!

Large organisations

Banks, building societies, local authorities, utilities, insurance companies – sometimes the problem is not so much getting your complaint dealt with as getting through to someone sensible in the first place. Many so-called helplines seem to be completely automated: 'If you are calling about XYZ, press 1. If you are calling about ABC, press 2...' When you press 1 you get another recorded voice with another list of options. And you are treated – at enormous expense, because this is going on your phone bill, not theirs – to synthesised music played very slightly off key.

One ploy to avoid getting caught in the automated loop,— a ploy which sometimes works – but not always – is to pretend *not* to have a touch tone telephone. This will sometimes – but not always – get you connected with a human being as, in the absence of input from you, your call may be re-routed to an operator. Please don't sue us if it doesn't work for you!

Sometimes the best tactic is to ignore the so-called helpline and find the number of the main office (Directory Enquiries, if all else fails). Call the switchboard (see *Go to the top* on page xx) and find out who is who – head of customer services, managing director or whatever – and get their names and extension numbers. That way you can bypass the automation and the Vivaldi. This can be quite demanding if an organisation is not keen to be contacted; see the letter about the dodgy curtain pole on page 102.

Once you are in contact with a human being, it is vital to get their names and to take good notes. See *Be organised*! on page 85 below. Then follow up your call with a letter.

Ombudsmen for all occasions

All the big organisations are subject to various controls, and there are regulatory bodies which will adjudicate in disputes on their particular patch. You will find a list of these in *Useful Contacts* on page 154.

Goods

Look at the diagram below. It shows the first stage of complaining about faulty goods.

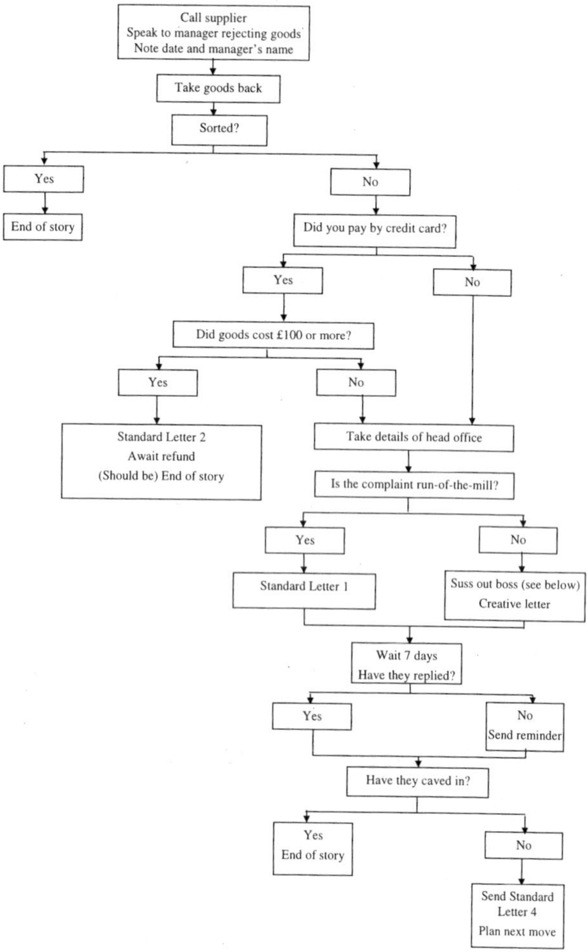

Step 1

Please refer again to the diagram. If you bought an item in a shop, your first move should be to telephone the shop and speak to the manager. Do this with a pen and a clean sheet of paper in front of you.

Make a careful note of the manager's name: you will need it later. Tell the manager your tale of woe and make it clear that you are rejecting the goods. They will of course ask you to bring in the item (unless it is something heavy or bulky like a fridge – though you may wish, for reasons of strategy, to bring it in anyway: see below). When you do turn up at the shop they will already be aware of your complaint and you won't have to go through it all with an underling.

Step 2

When you do go to the shop, armed of course with your receipt (strictly speaking it is not necessary, but in the real world, you are unlikely to get any redress without some proof of purchase) and any other paperwork, ask for the manager by name. Smile pleasantly. After all, the poor soul did not make the item personally, and has a job to do like everyone else.

'Hello. I'm .... We spoke earlier.' State your grievance politely and firmly and say what you want (replacement or refund). Usually that will be that and you will go home well pleased.

Most people find complaining in person fairly stressful. You will function better if you are feeling confident and at ease with yourself. We aren't talking power dressing here, but if you look well groomed you will feel confident and the manager will pick up your vibes and realise you are a force to be reckoned with.

If they get awkward

If the manager tries to weasel out, murmur 'Sale of Goods Act 1979', repeat your request and stand your ground. You should get what you want without an unpleasant scene.

Most independent traders will want to keep your custom and goodwill. If you are in the right, they will realise you mean business and are likely to capitulate without a struggle.

If the shop is part of a chain, the manager may not have the same incentive to keep your goodwill, and you may have to go higher up the line of command. If the faulty item is at all bulky or heavy, consider leaving it at the shop, making sure you are given a signed and dated receipt. We know a couple who took a faulty tumble dryer back to the shop and left it in the middle of the floor while discussing the problem – politely but animatedly – with the manager. It was a Saturday morning and he was only too delighted to see reason and replace the faulty appliance from stock. This course of action takes bottle, a suitable vehicle (though it is amazing what will fit into a small hatchback) and a willingness to make an exhibition of oneself in the interests of truth and right!

If you do not get satisfaction at this stage, remain pleasant, but do not leave the shop without obtaining full details of their head office. If they can give you the managing director's name and telephone number too, all the better.

A note on distance sales

If you bought by mail order or on the Internet, you can hardly march into a shop and demand your rights. Fortunately distance selling is heavily regulated and really serious problems are relatively uncommon. Start by calling the contact number in the information that came with the goods. A swift telephone call is usually all it takes. If things get nasty, however, you can use your low cunning to obtain the boss's name, fax number, etc (see *Go to the top* on page 83) and go on from there: all the tips and techniques apply.

At this stage, if the item cost £100 or more and you paid by credit card, you can use Standard Letter 2 to claim a refund. Remember to check your next statement to see if your refund went through.

Paying by credit card may encourage extravagance and debt, but when it comes to getting your money back, it is a sound move!

Step 3: Choose your weapon

If you didn't pay by credit card you will have to organise that refund for yourself. There are two ways of handling the next stage, depending on

- how cross you are and
- how unusual and/or interesting your complaint is.

The first weapon is Standard Letter 1 on page 124, which you can download from our website. All our standard letters are legally sound, though rather lacking in flair, and they say everything you need to say. You will not go far wrong if you use them while following the advice below. There are some broadly similar letters on the OFT website: details in *Useful Contacts* on page 139.

Probable effect

When Standard Letter 1 arrives in the post room of head office, it will be referred to Customer Services/Client Care (or whatever they are calling it this week). They will have seen many letters of complaint, some more persuasive than others, and they will have strict instructions about handling them.

The fact that you

- do not waffle
- give precise details of your purchase and
- state clearly what you want

will gain you some grudging respect – they are used to wading through six-page tirades to get to the nitty gritty and will appreciate your succinctness.

The fact that you mention the Sale of Goods Act 1979 will show that you know your rights and mean business.

The fact that you mention court proceedings should start a few alarm bells ringing.

If you are indeed on firm ground legally, Standard Letter 1 should get you a swift refund or replacement and an apology for the inconvenience you have been caused.

If they seem slow in replying, use the standard reminder, which of course applies to all your letters, standard or custom-made. Then, in the unlikely event that they either ignore you or give you a dusty answer, you can consider further action. See *If they still won't see reason* on page 89 below.

Go to the top

Standard Letter 1 is fine if it is an open and shut case and you have suffered no additional stress or inconvenience, but your complaint may not be a simple one. You may, by the time you write to head office, have been messed about to a quite unreasonable extent, and be feeling so aggrieved that a mere refund may not be enough. (An example is the letter on page 102 about the dodgy curtain pole.) That is when you might decide to bypass Customer Services and go straight to the top.

Probable effect

The boss may be unaware that customers are being treated unfairly. The Customer Services team normally deal with complaints. Your letter may be the first indication the boss has that someone further down the chain (ie the manager of the store where you bought your faulty goods) isn't doing a good job, and the boss is likely to be a lot more concerned than anyone in Customer Services would be. You will never know what the MD said or did to that manager, and it would be most improper for you to know, but if it improves his handling of complaints you will have done other consumers a favour...

Do your homework

For your letter to reach the top instead of being referred down to Customer Services, you need the name of the head of the organisation, probably the managing director. If the manager of the shop has not provided this, telephone the main switchboard at head office, act as naïve as your self-esteem will allow, and ask for the MD's name. If this is not forthcoming, ask to speak to the MD's secretary. Exchange first names, make friends with her, then say, '[Tania], my boss needs to get in touch with your boss. What's his/her name, please? And the extension number? And the fax line? Thank you. Have a nice day...'

Make a careful note of the MD's details and of the secretary's name. (You may wish to name-drop in later conversations: '[Tania] was so helpful...'.) Make a note of the date and time of the conversation for your file.

Now consider whether your first approach should be a telephone call, or a letter or fax. We'd favour something in writing, because your written complaint can then go on their file and (hopefully) be copied to the branch manager who has done you wrong with a demand to be told what the heck is going on.

Be organised!

These guidelines apply whichever route you take, and whatever you are complaining about.

If you telephone

- Start with a clean sheet of paper.
- Make a note beforehand of what you need to say.
- Write the date and time at the top of your sheet of paper.
- Have receipts and other documentation to hand.
- Make sure you get the name of the person you talk to, get them to spell it out if necessary, and write it down.
- Make it clear that you are rejecting the item and will be returning it shortly for a refund/replacement.
- Make a brief note of the telephone conversation. You may think that in a week's time you will remember the entire conversation in detail. You won't, but your notes will remind you.

Legal Lore

Lawyers take careful note of their telephone conversations both with clients and with 'the other side'. These contemporaneous jottings are called attendance notes or file notes, and are typed up to go on the file with the correspondence and other paperwork. Attendance notes have legal force and are a vital part of the documentation of a case. If you have to go to court your notes will have evidential value too.

If you write

If you are using a standard letter, use 'Dear Sir' and 'Yours faithfully'. If you know the recipient's name (see above, page 84), you can use 'Dear Mr/Ms [Brown]' and 'Yours sincerely'. This is more compelling than 'Dear Sir' and 'Yours faithfully', and much more difficult to send down to Customer Care with a scribbled 'Please sort'.

Give your correspondence credibility:

- Plain white A4 paper is best. Lined paper of any kind is naffsville.
- Your address and other contact details should go centre top – see Standard Letter 1 for the correct layout.
- Typed/word processed letters are easier to read than even the most beautiful handwriting.
- Honorifics (as in 'Yours faithfully, *Mrs* F. Vole') are naff. You sign yourself Harry Brown or Rosemary Border, and they write to you as Mr Brown or Ms Border.

- Omit your honours and academic qualifications unless they are relevant to the matter in hand.
- Solecisms are a dead giveaway. If your spelling is less than bombproof and your PC does not boast a spellchecker, use a dictionary. Nothing undermines your credibility like a few 'recieves' or 'definates'.

Your checklist

Whether you write Standard Letter 1 or something creative of your own, the following points are indispensable. Before you send a letter, go down the checklist to make sure you haven't omitted anything.

- Always give a *precise description* of the item with model number, etc if relevant ☐
- Say *when* you bought it ☐
- *Where* you bought it ☐
- *How much* it cost ☐
- Explain *briefly* what is wrong ☐
- *First contact*: say whom you spoke to initially (this is where the manager's name comes in handy) and when ☐
- Mention your Sale of Goods Act *rights* ☐
- Say clearly what you want done about the problem (Refund? Replacement? Compensation for any loss the faulty item has caused you? – see FAQs for inspiration. And resist the temptation to ask for anything unreasonable, such as the public flogging of the store manager who offended you) ☐
- Give a telephone number where you can be reached ☐

Then:

- Make photocopies of any receipts or documentation to enclose with your letter.
- Open a (paper) file and keep originals and copies of everything there.
- Mark in your diary the date you wrote, and if you do not get a reply within seven days, write a standard reminder enclosing a copy of your original letter (see page 126).

We like your style...

One of Shakespeare's more tedious characters said, 'Brevity is the soul of wit' before rambling on at great length. Do as he says, not as he does, and keep *your* letter brief. You are not being paid by the word and you are writing to a busy person with a full in-tray. Unless yours is a complex complaint (in which case consider a short covering letter with a more detailed report, preferably numbered and referenced), keep it down to one sheet of A4. And use the checklist!

You may like to start with something along the lines of 'I am sure you will be as disappointed/distressed/disturbed as I am to learn...'. That implies the recipient is dedicated to giving a good service and will be devastated by any failure to provide it.

You may also like to try a little gentle flattery along the lines of 'This is not the standard of service/quality I have come to expect from your firm and I am sure you will share my concern...'.

A touch of pathos and/or humour will not come amiss. Stand back from the problem and ask yourself how Dickens would have described the incident, then sum it up in a couple of sentences: 'Imagine my confusion and embarrassment when...' 'Picture for yourself the family gathered round...'. Senior managers receive a lot of boring letters, why not brighten up their day with yours?

Finally, if the thought of tackling the Big Boss unnerves you, picture him or her in the bath or on the loo, or wearing a silly hat. You are, after all, dealing with another human being with hopes and fears and frailties.

If they still won't see reason

This comes out as a jingle:

If they still won't play ball,
You have two ports of call.
Trading Standards is free,
But the courts charge a fee.

No, we shan't give up our day jobs just yet! In fact, before you even consider going to court you can try a trade organisation or an ombudsman. You can find a long list of useful organisations and another of ombudsmen in *Useful Contacts* on pages 154–155.

Legal Lore

Ombudsman is a Swedish word meaning *commissioner*. The ombudsman's duty is to protect the rights of the citizen against infringement of any kind. Sweden has had them since 1809; Britain appointed its first ombudsman, officially termed the Parliamentary Commissioner for Administration, in 1967.

Another option, if you really want to play dirty, is your local newspaper, which may well have a consumer-oriented journalist on the staff and might welcome the opportunity of taking up your case and/or filling a few column inches with your story. Readers respond readily to such stories and a good consumer grievance could run and run with minimal effort on the journalist's part and maximum embarrassment to the offending trader. That line of attack may not get you what you want, however, so keep it in reserve.

Note that we don't advocate *Watchdog*. This is not because it isn't a splendid programme – it is. But how many complaints do they receive, and how many can they actually do justice to on TV? Also, local journalists have local knowledge and are often more vicious about dodgy dealings on their patch.

See you in court

First of all, a word of reassurance. You may not need to go to court at all. A 'red warning' – a letter saying that you will sue unless the other person pays up – is often enough to get you what you want.

At the time of writing the Government is proposing a pre-action protocol which all litigants must follow, or risk losing their claims for costs (as opposed to the amount actually claimed). To avoid falling foul of the rules, you *must* write what lawyers call, variously, a letter of claim and a letter before action. This is in fact quite straightforward and we provide a sample, Standard Letter 4, on page 129.

You should, strictly speaking, start proceedings in the 'home court' of the person or organisation that owes you. This is the court nearest to the home, or principal place of business, of the defendant. However, they can, if they defend your claim, themselves take steps to have the case transferred to their 'home' court; and meanwhile you can get all the free advice you need from your local court.

Court officials are very good at form-filling. It is worth taking your paperwork in to your local court and asking a friendly clerk to check it for you.

The nitty gritty - filling in the claim form

The first thing to do is to fill in a claim form, Form N1, which is shown on the website. You can find a worked example on page 118, where Mr Lucky is claiming for compensation for his ruined holiday, but this one is what the greetings card manufacturers call 'blank for your own message'.
You can find a similar blank claim form on the court website, www.courtservice.gov.uk.

1. In the...

The name of the court should include the words 'County Court' (eg Ipswich County Court).

2. Claim number

Do not fill in the Claim Number box – the court will allocate a number to your case and fill in this box for you.

3. Claimant

You are the claimant, and this is where you fill in your name and address.

—If you are under 18, you will need an adult, for example a parent, to help you with the claim. The adult is called your litigation friend. After your name, add 'suing by his/her litigation friend' and insert your litigation friend's name. The litigation friend has to fill in another court form (not provided in this book but obtainable from the court), promising to pay any money that the court may order you to pay the debtor in the course of the proceedings (for example, costs).

4. Defendant

On the claim form the person who owes you – let's call them 'the debtor' for convenience – is referred to as the defendant. This is where you put their name and address. Take great care to get their name right.

- If the debtor is an individual, specify Mr/Mrs/Miss/Ms, etc as appropriate, provide first names if you know them, or initials otherwise, and surname.
- If the debtor is a sole trader and uses another name for their business, write in their own name, then the words 'trading as', followed by their trade name.
- If the debtor is a firm (two or more people in business together), write in the firm name followed by the words 'a firm'.
- If the debtor is a limited company, give the name of the company and the company registration number.

You can get a company registration number by doing a free search on the Companies House website www.companieshouse.gov.uk.

Insert the debtor's address, preferably including the postcode.

- For a private individual, use the debtor's home address.
- For a business debtor, use their principal place of business.

If the address is outside England and Wales, you must take professional advice because this book deals only with England and Wales.

5. Brief details of claim

You can keep this short and simple. Just make it clear what the claim is for.

6. Value

This box is for those who are unable to put a definite value on their claim. If you know how much is owed to you, leave this box blank and instead put the amount in the 'Amount claimed' box – see note 8.

7. Defendant's name and address

There is another box at the bottom of the claim form for the defendant's name and address.

- If you are suing one person only, repeat the name and address of the defendant in this box.
- If you are suing more than one person (eg three partners in a building firm), you will need a separate

form for each defendant. Put in the names of *all* the defendants at the top of each form, and use the box at the bottom of each form to give the name and address of *each* defendant separately. You will need to repeat all the information about the particulars of the claim on each form.

8. Amount claimed

Complete this box when you are claiming a fixed amount, eg a straightforward refund. If the precise amount of your claim is not known, complete the 'Value' box instead (note 6).

9. Court fee

The court fee is on a sliding scale according to value as follows:

Amount claimed not more than (£)	Fee (£)
200	27
300	38
400	50
500	60
1,000	80
5,000	115
15,000	230
50,000	350
50,000+	500

10. Solicitor's costs

As you are a litigant in person – that is, acting for yourself – you cannot claim solicitor's costs. Put N/A here.

11. Total amount

This is the amount you are claiming, plus the court fee.

12. Issue date

The court will complete the issue date.

13. Particulars of claim

Tell the court how the debt arose. Keep it brief – unless you anticipate the claim will be defended, in which case you need to get your story in first!

Give brief details of the contract terms:

- the date of contract;
- the type of contract (whether written or oral);
- the nature of goods or services provided;
- the price;
- other relevant terms.

You should also provide details such as invoice number, the date, the invoice amount, etc.

If you have a written contract, you should attach a copy. Also attach a copy of any expert reports.

Then explain, clearly but briefly, what is wrong – defects, problems, etc.

14. Statement of truth

This allows the facts set out in the Particulars of Claim to be treated as evidence. Write in your name clearly and sign.

15. Claimant's or claimant's solicitor's address

This address box is meant for claimants' solicitors. You do not need to use this box as long as your address on the front of the form is the one you want the court to use.

Now what?

Take or post to the court:

- one copy per defendant of the completed claim form, plus one copy for the court; and
- the court fee.

You can pay in cash (in which case use registered post or deliver personally), or by cheque made out to HMPG (Her Majesty's Paymaster General).

Keep a copy of the claim form(s) for your file.

The court will now – provided you got your form-filling right – issue your claim form (put an official stamp on it) and serve it on the debtor.

Service

The court normally posts the issued claim form to the defendant. At the same time, the court sends you a form called *Notice of Issue (Specified Amount) and Request for Judgment*. The form tells you the date of service, ie the date on which, according to the court rules, the debtor is deemed to have received the claim form. According to the court, first-class post takes two days. So, if the court posts the claim form, the date of service is two days after posting.

You may be able to speed up the procedure if you are prepared to serve the issued claim form yourself, *but*:

- a tricky defendant may deny ever receiving the claim form; and
- within seven days after the date of service you *must* notify the court of the date and method of service, using Form N215 (included in this book on pages 131–132). *If you do not send Form N215 to the court you cannot get judgment.*

If you want to serve the claim form yourself, collect the defendant's copy of the issued claim form from the court, or ask them to send it back to you.

You can serve it by:

- delivery to the defendant's address. Personal service (see *Buzzwords*) is not necessary; it is sufficient to put the claim form through the debtor's letterbox. Make a note of the day you delivered the claim form. The date of service, according to court rules, will be the day *after* you delivered the claim form;
- fax – in which case keep your transmission sheet;
- e-mail.

Response time

The debtor must respond within the time limit specified on the claim form, which – as long as you have filled in the Particulars of Claim on the claim form – is 14 days after the date of service (see above).

The significance of the response time is that if the debtor fails to respond by the deadline, you can get a walkover (see *Getting a default judgment* on page 101). So mark the deadline in your diary – and get in quick if the opportunity arises.

Many large organisations decide at this stage to cut their losses because defending a small claim is going to cost them more than paying up. They will either ignore your claim altogether (and enable you to get a *default judgment* – see below) or admit the claim and pay up, in which case you get a *judgment on admission*. In either case you won't have to go to court.

What can the debtor do?

The debtor communicates with the court (not with you), although any payments they make will come direct to you.

The debtor can:

- *Pay you in full*. End of story.
- *Admit the full amount of your claim, and offer to pay*. You can now apply for a judgment on admission; and this may be an attractive option if you find the debtor's payment proposals unacceptable.
- *Lie low and say nothing*. If the debtor does not respond to the claim form before the deadline, you can apply for a default judgment (a sort of legal walkover, where the other side rolls over and has its tummy tickled) for the whole amount.
- *Admit part of the claim, disputing the balance*. You can now apply for a judgment for the admitted amount only.
- *Dispute the whole of the claim*. You cannot now apply for a default judgment, but if the debtor's grounds for dispute have, as the court rules put it, 'no real prospect of success', you may still be able to get a summary judgment (see *Buzzwords*).
- *Make a claim against you*. If so, you may still be able to get a default judgment if the debtor's claim is not a defence to the debt. You will, however, still have to defend the debtor's claim against you (outside the scope of this book; seek professional advice).

Getting a default judgment

If you are entitled to a default judgment, the day after the deadline, complete the Request for Judgment part of the Notice of Issue which the court has sent you.

Sign and date the form and return it to the court. There is no fee and you do not have to attend court.

The court will now send you your judgment, and also send copies to the defendant and the Register of County Court Judgments. Well done!

Be organised!

- Always quote the case number on all your correspondence with the court.
- Always keep copies of all written communications, both with the debtor and with the court.
- Always keep file notes, with dates, of all meetings and telephone conversations.

Some creative complaints

Every one of these is genuine.

The dodgy curtain pole

This one follows all our guidelines. It states clearly what the item was, where and when purchased and for how much. It names and shames. It has a touch of humour; and it states clearly what the writer is asking for. The MD kept this lady's goodwill. Sadly, the manager of the store concerned hides when she goes in.

Letter

Date: 31 March [ ]
Mr ....
Managing Director, [ ] Ltd
Fax no ....

Dear Mr ....

I am writing to you because I have so far failed to obtain satisfaction from your [ ] store or from your customer care department. I am sure you will be as distressed as I am to learn how badly I have been treated.

On 4 January [ ] I bought a wooden curtain pole, price £14.99, at the [ ] branch of your store. I am copying the receipt to you. When I came to unpack it, I discovered that three metal plates with screws were missing. I drove the 15 miles to your [ ] branch with the item and spoke with your Mr ...., carefully showing him the instructions and explaining what was missing. He did not have another pole in stock but promised to get the missing parts sent from another branch without delay.

After several weeks and numerous telephone calls – and long after I had become tired of looking at an uncurtained window and bought another curtain pole elsewhere – a package arrived with the wrong parts, in the wrong colour. I called the store and pointed this out to Mr .... and suggested he ought to make amends, preferably with a bunch of flowers, as I had wasted much time, energy and fuel as well as the original cost of the curtain pole. He never got back to me.

Becoming a little impatient, I called and asked for the telephone number of your head office. They promised to call back, but never did. I then asked Directory Enquiries, who did not have your head office listed but gave me a Swansea number. I called it and spoke to Mr ...., who promised to pass the matter to a Ms.................... in Customer Care for action. More than two weeks have passed and I have heard nothing from her.

I have just telephoned your head office and obtained your name and fax number and I am writing to invite you to call or fax me before close of business today, failing which I will discuss this matter with our local Trading Standards Department. I find it hard to believe that it is company policy to ignore dissatisfied customers. It seems to me that your firm owes me:

an explanation; an apology; the cost of the (useless) curtain pole; the cost of two (fruitless) 30-mile round trips; the cost of my telephone calls and faxes; something in respect of the annoyance and inconvenience I have suffered. And a bunch of flowers would not come amiss!

Yours sincerely

Result: Telephone call within the hour, apology, promise to investigate the delays, etc, bouquet of flowers and £50 voucher.

All sound and no suction

A lady bought a vacuum cleaner which made a great deal of noise but refused to pick up anything. The store manager was unsympathetic. This piece of doggerel faxed to the MD's own line got results.

A lady bought a vacuum,
It cost her sixty pound,
But when she tried to use it,
This is what she found.
She plugged it in and switched it on,
It made an awful row.
But would it pick up anything?

Nohow!
She took it back to [Bloggs's],
Who'd sold her the machine,
She said, 'It makes a lot of noise
But does not clean.'
The manager said, 'Nonsense,
It's working – hear it roar!' -
She left the faulty cleaner there
And marched out of the store.
She found your name and number -
She had to ask around -
And if you know what's good for you
You'll send her sixty pound!

Result: A refund, a £20 voucher and a friendly phone call from the MD, who said she'd made his day.

Duff batteries that ruined an experiment

This letter follows all the guidelines – date and place of purchase, etc, a touch of humour – except one: it leaves the matter of compensation open to negotiation. Read on and you will see why. Note the writer lists his degrees. This is because they are relevant to the matter in hand. Otherwise to list them would be showing off, of the most obnoxious kind.

Letter

Mr....................
Managing Director
.... Limited

Dear Sir

Your Batteries

I am a cave radio enthusiast. There being few power points in caves, I rely completely on batteries to power all my equipment. In preparation for our twice-yearly Cave Radio and Electronics Group weekend of the [date], I bought a set of 10 C size .... batteries at [shop details] at a total cost of £18. I specifically chose .... because in my experience they last a great deal longer than other batteries.

The cells were to run an Amstrad PPC640D portable computer. Previous experience with your batteries suggested that I could expect between 10 and 14 hours' use. To my intense disappointment, and to the detriment of the entire experiment, these batteries gave just half an hour of power, which according to my calculations works out at £36 per hour. After that time the computer repeatedly re-booted itself and failed. The *off*-load voltage had dropped to less than 1.4 V per cell.

The cells were replaced by an external 12 volt lead-acid battery which was about half-charged (note that the computer, according to its manual, needs 15 V rather than the 12–14 V that the lead-acid battery was supplying). The computer did, however, work properly. As the on-load voltage of the alkaline cells must have been about the same as the lead-acid battery, it would seem that your product did not deliver the peak current needed during computer start-up.

As this is so contrary to my previous experience with your products, I begin to wonder whether the cells which I bought were in fact counterfeit. I am therefore enclosing one cell and two of the packages. You will note that one of them says *Install by* [date] and the other says *Install by* [date] so there is no question of their being past their sell-by date.

You may gather that I am very perturbed about this indeed. An £18 refund will in no way put right the fact that (there being no limestone caves in Suffolk) I made a 500 mile round trip to conduct experiments, and that my work was jeopardised by faulty batteries.

I look forward to your comments.

Yours faithfully

Eur Ing .... MPhil, DipEE, CEng, MIEE, MBCS

Result: Two fresh sets of batteries, an apology and a description of the investigations which his letter had prompted.

A load of old rubbish

The writer of this letter was incensed because a neighbour was charged £8 for dumping her hedge clippings, on the grounds that they constituted 'trade waste'.

Letter

Date:
Fao Mr ....
Waste Disposal
County Hall
....
Fax no ....

Dear Mr ....

My Garden Rubbish

We spoke on 21 August, just before you went on holiday, and I promised to fax you. I thought I'd give you the opportunity to settle in and clear your in-tray before bothering you and enclosing a copy of the receipt for £8 which I believe was wrongly charged in the belief that my hedge clippings constituted trade waste.

You told me that there had been a clampdown on what you called 'unauthorised trade waste', and I warmly support this. It seems to me, however, that you must be using some arcane definition of 'trade waste' of which most people are unaware. I have always understood trade waste to be waste generated by tradesmen such as builders, professional landscape gardeners or plumbers, who generate a lot of rubbish in the course of their trade and for whom the cost of its disposal is a tax-deductible expense. We generated a lot of spoil when we dug our swimming pool 15 years ago and, if we had not found a farmer who collected it to fill a hole on his land, the bill for disposal would have been considerable – and rightly so.

As I explained to you, the waste for which £8 was 'extorted' was not in that league. We had trimmed our hedges and Mr .... kindly took the clippings to the dump for me. I gave him a piece of beef to thank him. I would be surprised if the County Solicitor were to argue that this small gift converted the clippings from ordinary domestic or garden refuse into trade waste, but perhaps you had better ask him:

a) for clear, unambiguous definitions of domestic waste and trade waste;
b) whether a small piece of brisket of beef transforms a good neighbour into a tradesman;
c) whether you slipped up by failing to inform the public before 'moving the goalposts', to give them the chance to put their garden waste into green sacks for free collection by the dustmen;
d) whether you should now write to all Council Tax payers alerting them to the change in the rules.

Meanwhile I look forward to your cheque for the £8.

Yours sincerely

Result: A cheque for £8 but no apology. Nor indeed any answers to points a) to d). Well, that's local government for you, innit?

Money in limbo

The writer of this letter tried to open a savings account with a cheque for £1,000. It was easier said than done and several people made some quite astonishing booboos. Note how important it is to get people's names and take good file notes.

Date: 2 December.............
Ms...........................
.... Personal Finance

Dear Ms ....

Thank you for your letter of yesterday's date enclosing a cheque for £1,007.34 representing my original investment of £1,000 plus the interest it would have earned.

I am a little puzzled, as

a) as long ago as November 14 Ms Melanie P............... in your Bristol office told me that she had ordered a cheque that day;

b) yesterday Ms Pauline S................ – also, I think, in your Bristol office – told me she had made enquiries and been told that a cheque had been posted on 24 November;

c) although the cheque is dated 24 November, your letter was dated, and the envelope postmarked, 1 December, *after my telecon with Ms S...............*

Ms S ...., whom I found sensible and helpful throughout, has made careful enquiries and kept good file notes and it looks as though someone else in your organisation was less than frank with her.

I have on file full documentary evidence of a most unsatisfactory standard of service, including

a) delay in acknowledging my initial cheque for £1,000;

b) failure to provide an opening statement with the welcome pack which eventually arrived;

c) an error on 2 November by 'Sarah' who, perhaps prudently, refused to give her surname, in setting up security procedures which resulted in problems thereafter for everyone who tried to deal with me over the telephone;

d) failure to respond correctly to my initial letter of complaint: in the reply, which was clearly a form letter kept on file for all occasions, the writer got the date of the complaint wrong and failed to address any of the points in my letter;

e) failure to respond to repeated requests for the account to be closed and my money returned.

During these goings-on I received two apologetic telephone calls (both of course documented here) and a further form letter with a £20 voucher (the caller initially offered £10, I roared with laughter and she obtained her supervisor's permission to offer £20).

Please see, enclosed, my original letter of complaint, dated 2 November and never properly answered. I write from personal experience of fielding complaints, and I fully realise that you personally had no part in this sorry tale. As Customer Relations Team Leader, however, you do have a duty to try to put matters right and I look forward to hearing from you.

Yours sincerely

Result: the money returned with interest, a £20 voucher and a huge bouquet of flowers.

Grounded!

This is quite an interesting complaint, in that the complainer was also able to extort (after a struggle) compensation from the travel insurance company in respect of flight delay. The travel insurers tried to weasel out because the flight was between two US airports and therefore, they said, internal. The complainer shot them down in flames and got the money.

Note how well documented this letter is.

Letter

Ms ....
Customer Care Manager
.............Airlines

Dear Ms ....

Flight no .... 1830 hours Boston to Nashville ....: (names of passengers)

I would normally have written to you immediately after our return, but I caught something on the .... Airlines flight to Heathrow last week and have been ill ever since. I suppose that if several hundred people are crammed into a tin can for eight hours and the air they breathe is recycled, someone is bound to pick up an infection! Anyway, I apologise for not contacting you at once. You might say that the delay has given me the opportunity of reflecting on my experience and deciding that yes, I am still very angry indeed and that yes, it is worth complaining.

As I am sure you know, on the evening of .... a great many flights out of Logan Airport, Boston, were either delayed or cancelled, and ours was one of those affected. We turned up in good time for our 1830 flight to Nashville and were told it was expected to be on time. Later, the news came that the flight was delayed. Finally, at 2045, over two hours after scheduled takeoff time, we were told to board the aircraft. We did so, and taxied around for another hour, then the pilot announced that if we took off the crew would exceed their permitted hours. We were taken back to the airport at 2200 to await a 1030 flight next morning. *Wouldn't it be sensible to think about flying hour regulations before you load people onto your aircraft?*

We spent 45 minutes at the help desk, where nobody seemed able to realise that the reason for the cancellation was flight hours (their problem), not weather conditions (God's). I asked politely for meal vouchers and a place to stay for the night, but was told by Mr........... that the airline was not responsible for delays due to bad weather. Finally a senior member of staff, Mrs......................, appeared and confirmed that the reason for the cancellation was in fact flying hours. This of course made the airline responsible for doing something to help us.

After a further 30 minutes' delay we were issued with meal vouchers (although the only food outlet which was still open was Dunkin Donuts) and Mrs................ called an accommodation agency to find us somewhere to stay. We were then issued with hotel vouchers and breakfast vouchers, and after a further 30 minutes' delay we were bussed to the .... Inn at Hyannis Port. By the time we arrived there (have you looked at the map lately? It is not a short trip) it was well after midnight and everyone was tired and upset. We were faced with boarding the bus again at 7.30 a.m. next morning for our 1030 flight.

It seems you used .... to book the hotel. They owe you an apology, because they failed to inform the .... Inn that we were coming.

So, when we arrived at the .... Inn after a long bus ride in the dark, the desk staff were not expecting us. It was after 1.30 a.m. before they finally agreed that we had a right to be there, accepted our vouchers and allocated us rooms. There was of course nothing to eat or drink.

In the morning the hotel laid on coffee in the foyer but their restaurant did not open until after 7 a.m. It was waitress service only and no buffet service was available (had nobody on reception that night left a message that a buffet was needed in the morning?). This meant that we could not use our breakfast vouchers at the hotel, and had to face the bus ride back to Logan on empty stomachs before breakfasting as best we could at the airport café. When we did board the onward flight to Nashville, there was a final annoyance in store: there were not even enough lunchboxes to go round (*don't you count your passengers and make sure each has a lunchbox?*) and my husband and I had to share one.

When we reached Nashville, a day late, we decided, in view of our traumatic experience on the way there, to stay an extra day there with our friends, which meant changing the Nashville-Chicago leg of our return from Monday .... to Tuesday .... I am sure you will be as concerned as I am to learn that it took over an hour to perform this simple transaction, using your helpline. The assistant, Mr..............., who finally changed the booking demanded two $189 supplements and wanted my credit card number to extort them. I warn you that if anything of the kind appears on my credit card statement I shall be very angry indeed.

My husband and I fly quite a lot, both on business and for pleasure. This was our first flight with .... Airlines; and recent experience suggests it is likely to be our last. I feel, however, that you have a right to tell me your side of the story and to offer to make amends, and I look forward to hearing from you. I am copying this letter to Cath Urquhart, Chief Travel Editor of *The Times*, who is aware of my concerns.

Yours sincerely

Result: $300 and a grovelling apology, and nobody did charge for the changes of schedule.

Desperate measures

There are times when the courteous, literate letter or the patient telephone call produce no result whatsoever. Then you can consider desperate measures. All of these stories are true, but the names have been changed.

The wayward washer

Mrs D bought a washing machine from a High Street retailer. It broke down within a day or two, filling the house with the fumes of melted plastic and scorched clothes. The shop sent a replacement machine, which flooded the kitchen. The shop manager sent an engineer who assured Mrs D it was a tiny fault and that he had fixed it. He hadn't. The machine broke down again. The store manager did his Rock of Gibraltar imitation.

Mrs D typed out a notice explaining briefly in unemotional, non-abusive terms what had happened. She stood outside the shop on a busy Saturday morning handing a copy to everyone who went in and out. When the store manager called the police she explained to the officer why she was there. A small crowd gathered. When the press arrived too, the store manager caved in and offered Mrs D a full refund. She stuck out for the cost of the ruined clothes and damaged floor as well.

Taking a hostage

This story appeared in *The Times* on 13 April 2001. Diane, frustrated at a 15-month delay in getting her faulty dishwasher fixed, took an engineer hostage until the suppliers offered her a new machine. Diane said, 'Normally I wouldn't say boo to a goose, but something inside me snapped. Without thinking, I just locked all my doors and told him he couldn't leave... I was shaking but I stood my ground.' The supplier said, 'In the interests of customer service we offered her a new machine.' Diane was probably breaking the law by keeping the man there against his will, but it would be a bold Crown Prosecutor who brought a case against her.

Flowers and grovels

Mrs F bought a flat and, as a shareholder in the property management company, attended an AGM and found herself voted in as a director. All went well until she received a letter from the company secretary, an accountant, saying that the letting agent responsible for managing the flats had disappeared with the company's books and everyone's money.

Mrs F contacted ...., the company's bank, and asked the manager to put a stop on the company's cheques. To cut a long story short, the manager behaved with breathtaking arrogance and Mrs F had to enlist the police to obtain bank statements (the manager had cited Data Protection, then when overruled tried to extort a three-figure sum for copying the statements to her) or even, initially, to persuade the manager to talk to her.

Mrs F did not bother claiming for her wasted time. Instead, once the manager had caved in, co-operated with the police and given Mrs F the information she needed, she demanded a bouquet of flowers and an apology. They duly arrived, whereupon Mrs F changed the company's bankers. She then pursued the rogue agent and had the satisfaction of seeing him sentenced to jail.

And finally, a holiday claim!

Worked example of Claim Form

Claim form [info]

In the: [defendant's local] County Court.
Claim no:

Claimant

Mr Cedric Lucky
4, South Street,
Dunmoanin,
Southampton.
SO4 5NY
01234 567890

Defendant(s)

Scarytours plc,
[Registered Office address]
11, High Street,
London.
NW1 3RE
Company no: 34567211

Brief details of claim

The Claimant claims damages for misrepresentation and breach of contract arising out of an agreement dated 31 October 2000 between the Claimant and the Defendant whereby the Defendant agreed to provide the Claimant and his family with a holiday in Portugal.

Value

The Claimant expects to recover not more than £5,000.

Defendant's name and address	**Amount claimed**
Scarytours plc, [Registered Office address] 11, High Street, London. NW1 3RE Company no: 34567211	**Court fee** £100 **Solicitor's costs** .... **Total amount** **Issue date** 25/06/01

Particulars of claim (attached/to follow)

IN THE [defendant's local] COUNTY COURT **Claim no:**

BETWEEN Mr Cedric Lucky CLAIMANT

and

Scarytours plc DEFENDANT

PARTICULARS OF CLAIM

1. At all material times the Defendant carried on business as a tour operator.

2. On or about the 1st October 2000 the Claimant acquired a copy of the Defendant's Spring Break brochure. The brochure included particulars of a holiday in Portugal and made the following representations about the holiday on page 94:

'the apartment block is set in a peaceful area. Every apartment has a sea view and use of a communal swimming pool'.

A copy of the relevant page is annexed to these Particulars of Claim.

3. In reliance on the information in the brochure, on the 31st October 2000 the Claimant, Cedric Lucky, entered into an agreement with the Defendant contained in or evidenced by a booking form (copy annexed to these Particulars of Claim), whereby the Defendant agreed to provide a holiday for a family of four for two weeks in an apartment in Portugal between 7th and 21st April 2001 inclusive

4. The total cost of the holiday was £1,799 which the Claimant paid to the Defendant by the 7th March 2001.

5. It was an implied term of the agreement that the apartment and the holiday would match the description contained in the brochure, such term being implied by section 6(1) of the Package Travel, Package Holidays and Package Tours Regulations 1992.

6. Further, the said descriptions were misrepresentations by which the Claimant was induced to enter the said contract

7. The said representations were false and the Defendant was in breach of contract in that the holiday and apartment did not conform to the brochure.

PARTICULARS

8.The claimant and his family arrived at the apartment on the 7th April 2001 to find that it was not located in a 'peaceful area' as stated in the brochure. It was in fact situated alongside a busy main road in a noisy, commercial area. The apartment was surrounded by bars and nightclubs which were commonly open until 3 or 4 a.m.

9. The swimming pool mentioned in the brochure had been filled in two years previously to make room for extra car parking facilities.

10. The Claimant's apartment did not have a sea view as stated in the brochure but instead overlooked the kitchens at the rear of the apartment block.

11. By reason of the said misrepresentations and breaches of contract, the Claimant has suffered loss and damage.

PARTICULARS

12. In addition to the cost of the holiday, the Claimant suffered additional expense to the sum of £146 in transporting his family to a nearby leisure centre every day and paying for entry so that his children could use the swimming pool facilities there.

13. Further by reason of these matters the Claimant and his family suffered considerable distress, anxiety, inconvenience and disappointment and will seek damages for distress.

PARTICULARS

14. As a result of the noise emanating from nearby bars and nightclubs into the early hours the Claimant and his family had difficulty sleeping. As a result the family became tired and irritable. The children consequently spent most of their holiday in tears.

15. The Claimant's wife suffered three migraines whilst on holiday, which she attributes to the noise and lack of sleep.

16. The Claimant claims interest under section 69 County Courts Act 1984 at such rate and over such period as the court thinks fit.

AND THE CLAIMANT CLAIMS

1. Damages for misrepresentation and breach of contract, to include damages for distress

2. Interest on the damages pursuant to section 69 of the County Courts Act 1984.

Statement of Truth
(I believe) the facts stated in these particulars of claim are true.

Full name Mr Cedric Lucky

Signed C. Lucky

Result: The maximum payable would be the full cost of the holiday (£1,799), depending on whether the court felt that the family had had any enjoyment from it, plus £146 for the consequential expenses plus, say, £300 for loss of enjoyment – but this is of course subjective.

Standard letters

Faulty goods

Standard Letter 1

Your address
Your postcode
Your telephone number, email, etc

Date:

For the attention of the Managing Director
Name of firm
Address of firm
Postcode

Dear Sir

Sale of Goods Act 1979

On [date] I bought [say (a) what you bought, with details of model no, etc, (b) where you bought it, (c) what it cost]. [Now say what is wrong with it]. On [date] I took the faulty item back to the shop and spoke with the manager, [give manager's name]. I asked him/her to refund my money, but he/she refused.

I enclose a copy of my receipt for ease of reference.

I am sure you are aware that under the Sale of Goods Act 1979 I have a right to expect the goods I purchase to be of satisfactory quality and fit for their purpose. The fact that [say here what was wrong with the goods] after so short a time would appear to demonstrate that the goods were inherently faulty when I bought them. It seems to me, therefore, that you are in breach of your contract and I am rejecting the goods and asking you to refund my money.

I look forward to hearing from you as soon as possible, and in any event within seven days of today's date, failing which I will consider taking action against you in the Small Claims Court. If you wish to discuss this matter, please feel free to contact me.

Yours faithfully

Standard reminder

If you decide to give them another chance to respond before you bring in the heavy artillery, you can send this reminder with a copy of your original letter.

Dear Sir

I wrote to you on [date] about [ ]. As I have not yet received a reply, I am wondering whether my original letter has gone astray. I enclose a copy for ease of reference and look forward to hearing from you shortly.

Yours faithfully

Seeking a refund from a credit card company

Note: This only works for purchases of £100 or over.

Standard Letter 2

Your address
Your postcode
Your telephone number, email, etc

Date:

Credit card company
Address
Postcode

Dear Sir

Consumer Credit Act 1974

On [date] I bought [say (a) what you bought, with details of model no, etc, (b) where you bought it, (c) what it cost]. [Now say what is wrong with it]. I purchased the goods with credit card no [credit card details] issued by you.

Sadly, [say what was wrong with the goods]. On [date] I took the faulty item back to the shop and spoke with the manager, [give manager's name]. I asked him/her to refund my money, but he/she refused. As it is clear that the item was faulty [details here] I believe that the seller is in breach of its contract. I also believe that under section 75 of the Consumer Credit Act 1974 you are jointly liable with the seller for any faults in the goods supplied.

I am therefore asking you please to credit my account with the sum of [price of goods] as soon as possible, but in any event within 14 days.

If you wish to discuss this matter please feel free to contact me.

Yours faithfully

Complaining about a service

Standard Letter 3

Your address
Your postcode
Your telephone number, email, etc

Date:

For the attention of the Managing Director
Name of firm
Address of firm
Postcode

Dear Sir

Your invoice number [or whatever]

I refer to the [describe service] you carried out for me on [date]. On [date] I noticed that the work was defective, only [ ] days after you completed it.

The defects in the work seem to be:

[detailed list of problems]

It was implied in the contract between us that you would carry out the work with reasonable skill and care and use materials of reasonable quality. As I am sure you know, I am entitled to expect this under the Sale of Goods and Services Act 1982. The faults listed above show that you have failed to carry out your obligations under the Act and I have a right to make a claim against you for breach of contract.

I am, however, while reserving my right to make a claim against you, allowing you the opportunity of putting the faults right within 14 days from today's date at your own expense. If you do not carry out this work within the specified time I shall ask another contractor to put the matter right and charge this work to you.

I enclose a copy of the invoice for ease of reference.

I look forward to hearing from you as soon as possible, and in any event within 14 days of today's date, failing which I will consider taking action against you in the Small Claims Court. If you wish to discuss this matter, please feel free to contact me.

Yours faithfully

Letter of claim

Standard Letter 4

Your address
Your postcode
Your telephone number, email, etc

Date:

For the attention of the Managing Director
Name of firm
Address of firm
Postcode

Dear

[*Here put something to identify the case, eg Faulty Washing Machine or Defective Workmanship]*

I refer to my letter[s] of [*dates*] and my claim for [*amount*], also to my reminder[s] of [*date[s]*]. I must ask you to settle this claim within seven days of today's date. If you fail to do so, I shall take legal action against you without further warning to recover the debt together with interest and costs. You should note that county court judgments are registered and may make it difficult for you to obtain credit in the future.

If you have difficulty in paying, please contact me immediately.

Yours [etc]

Certificate of Service

In the	
Claim No.	
Claimant	
Defendant	

On the *(insert date)*

the *(insert title or description of documents served)*

a copy of which is attached to this notice was served on *(insert name of person served, including position i.e. partner, director if appropriate)*

Tick as appropriate

- ☐ by first class post
- ☐ by Document Exchange
- ☐ by delivering to or leaving
- ☐ by handing it to or leaving it with
- ☐ by fax machine (time sent)
  (you may want to enclose a copy of the transmission sheet)
- ☐ by e-mail
- ☐ by other means *(please specify)*

at *(insert address where service effected, include fax or DX number or e-mail address)*

being the defendant's:

- ☐ residence
- ☐ registered office
- ☐ place of business
- ☐ other *(please specify)*

The date of service is therefore deemed to be *(insert date – see over for guidance)*

I confirm that at the time of signing this Certificate the document has not been returned to me as undelivered.

Signed
(Claimant)(Defendant)('s Solicitor)('s Litigation friend)

Position or office held
(if signing on behalf of firm or company)

Date

TSO 2 N215: 1 of 2

Notes for guidance

Please note that these notes are only a guide and are not exhaustive.
If you are in doubt you should refer to Part 6 of the rules.

Where to serve

Nature of party to be served	Place of service
Individual	• usual or last known residence
Proprietor of business	• usual or last known residence; or • place of business or last known place of business
Individual who is suing or being sued in the name of a firm	• usual or last known residence; or • principal or last known place of business of the firm
Corporation (incorporated in England and Wales) other than a company	• principal office of the corporation; or • any place of business within the jurisdiction where the corporation carries on its activities and which has a real connection with the claim
Company registered in England and Wales	• principal office of the company or corporation; or • any place of business of the company within the jurisdiction which has a real connection with the claim

Personal Service A document is served personally on an individual by leaving it with that individual. A document is served personally on a company or other corporation by leaving it with a person holding a senior position within the company or corporation. In the case of a partnership, you must leave it with either a partner or a person having control or management at the principal place of business. Where a solicitor is authorised to accept service on behalf of a party, service must be effected on the solicitor, unless otherwise ordered.

Deemed Service Part 6.7(1). A document which is served in accordance with these rules or any relevant practice direction shall be deemed to be served on the day shown in the following table.

Method of service	Deemed day of service
First class post	The second day after it was posted
Document exchange	The second day after it was left at the document exchange
Delivering the document to or leaving it at a permitted address	The day after it was delivered to or left at the permitted address
Fax	If it is transmitted on a business day before 4pm., on that day, or otherwise on the business day after the day on which it was transmitted.
Other electronic method	The second day after the day on which it was transmitted.

- If a document (other than a claim form) is served after 5pm on a business day, or at any time on a Saturday, Sunday or a bank holiday, the document shall, for the purpose of calculating any period of time after service of the document, be treated as having been served on the next business day.

- In this context "business day" means any day except Saturday, Sunday or a bank holiday; and "bank holiday" includes Christmas Day and Good Friday.

Service of documents on children and patients – The rules relating to service on children and patients are contained in Part 6.6 of the rules.

Claim Forms – The general rules about service are subject to the special rules about service of claim forms contained in rules 6.12 to 6.16.

TSO 2 N215: 2 of 2

Useful Contacts

The *Useful Contacts* sections in the other books in this series consist only of addresses, websites and telephone numbers mentioned in the text or suggested as sources of further information. There is no attempt at evaluation, because in general there is no choice. If you are setting up a limited company you need either the Companies House central helpline or their website on www.companieshouse.gov.uk and no other source will give you the information and official forms you need. A site may be slow to load, unhelpful or out of date (we hasten to add that Companies House is none of those things!) but it is all there is available.

With consumer affairs things are slightly different. There is a wealth of free information available, especially on the Internet. Some is official, and therefore legally sound, and some is emphatically not.

It is fair to say that you could have written this book yourself if you had time to surf all the relevant sites, take all the information on board, weed out the unreliable parts and collate it into a coherent whole. As it is, we have done all that for you and included the best in this book. We hope you have found the book useful and that you will find these sources of further information interesting and helpful.

Free information

Trading Standards Net

One excellent feature of this site is the alphabetical list of Useful Organisations, from the Advertising Standards Authority to the Textile Services Association. The site also lists all the different ombudsmen and provides several standard letters of complaint. The excellent '*TS Help! Just a click away*!' links you with advice on everything from pesticides to pushchairs, barbecues to bunk beds, and an excellent section on buying new and used cars.

The eight-page piece on Consumer Safety Legislation is informative rather than exciting, but it is worth printing off a copy to keep on file.

www.tradingstandards.net

Trading Standards Central

Trading Standards Central has a London Underground-style map as its heading. You click on a 'station' such as 'Safety Warnings'.

There are many free booklets to view on screen or print out. Ten out of ten for user-friendliness and even entertainment value.

www.tradingstandards.gov.uk

Food and the law

We recommend the *Foodsense* series of booklets, produced by the DEFRA and the Department of Health (DOH) Joint Food Safety and Standards Group (JFSSG). Examples are *Food Safety, Understanding Food Labels* and *Preventing Food Fraud.*

Call DEFRA Publications, tel 08459 556000, for free copies.

You can also access the Food Standards Agency website on www.foodstandards.gov.uk.

JFSSG also has a customer helpline on 020 7276 8000.

Further advice on food, including guidance on genetic modification, etc, is available on the *Food for our Future* website, produced by the Food and Drink Federation. You can get to it via www.consumer.gov.uk and this website will also take you to the *Foodlink* site, which is put together by the group of organisations responsible for Food Safety Week.

Gateway to good things

The *Consumer Gateway* website, which is run by the DTI (Department of Trade and Industry), offers online access to consumer information and advice and links to other websites run by government departments and consumer organisations. This may sound dull, but it is far from that. There is a great deal of good material on the site itself, the links take you to even more, and it is so readable as to be entertaining.

Their address is www.consumer.gov.uk

Good advice

The *Adviceguide* site was set up by the National Association of Citizens' Advice Bureaux. It is a good starting point for a search for advice on more arcane problem areas, some of which are not mentioned in this book. An example is neighbour trouble. Available on www.adviceguide.org.uk and www.nacab.org.uk

Lawyers on the Web

The *Consumer-solicitors* site gives a clear and readable guide to consumer law. Their welcome page includes a box invitingly labelled 'Get groaning here and let off some steam'. As the former editor of a popular *Groans and Gloats* column in a local newspaper, Rosy can imagine how popular that part of the site is, and how interesting the various groans must be.

Additionally, there is a search engine to locate a consumer-oriented solicitor near you. The address is: www.consumer-solicitors.co.uk

Holidays in hell

ABTA
020 7307 1907
Website: www.abta.com
Click on Building Confidence in Travel.

The *HolidayComplaint* site says it is building up an online database of holiday complaints. It gives advice on how to complain and says it will soon be providing consumers with a personal consultancy service. You can find out more about this service by e-mailing info@holidaycomplaint.com

This site is particularly good at naming and shaming the travel firms who disappoint their customers. It might save you a lot of grief if you checked out this site before booking your holiday, as it mentions the various resorts and hotels by name as well as the response (if any; some seem to have maintained a deafening silence) the tour operator made to the complaint. Some of the complainers have even set up their own websites to swap horror stories.

You can search by individual tour operators to see how many complaints have been made about them. Interestingly, as of 1 June 2001 Airtours had generated 35 complaints and Thomson 23, but Thomas Cook and Voyages Jules Verne only 2 and 1 respectively. The address is: www.holidaycomplaint.com

CAA (Civil Aviation Authority)/ATOL (Air Travel Organiser's Licensing)
Advice lines: 020 7453 6430, 020 7453 6360
Website: www.atol.org.uk
This site explains travellers' rights, lists companies which are part of the ATOL scheme and which have recently gone bust.

Air Transport Users' Council
Advice line: 020 7240 6061, 2 p.m.–5 p.m. weekdays
Website: www.auc.org.uk

Association of British Insurers
Offer a free leaflet about travel insurance.
Tel: 020 7600 3333
Website: www.abi.org.uk

Howtocomplain.com
www.howtocomplain.com

This is an interactive site which helps you to track down the relevant people and organisations to complain to – often online. They make the point that 'Organisations themselves welcome complaints...the opportunity to improve the service they provide and to retain customer loyalty'.

We found this site helpful and informative; and it is developing all the time.

OFT
www.oft.gov.uk

The *Office of Fair Trading* website offers, among other excellent things, a seven-page leaflet called *How to Complain*. It deals with both goods and services and offers many useful addresses. It even prints the scale of court fees if you decide to sue in the small claims court.

There are links with *Trading Standards Central* (see above), Oftel and British Ombudsmen.

The Banking Ombudsman Scheme
Financial Ombudsman Service
PO Box 4
South Quay Plaza
183 Marsh Wall
London E14 9SR

Consumer helpline: 0845 766 0902
Switchboard: 020 7404 9944
Fax: 020 7405 5052
Website: www.obo.org.uk
E-mail: banking.ombudsman@financial-ombudsman.org.uk

If your bank is bugging you, this should be your first port of call. They resolve individual complaints against banks in the UK. The service is free, but they can award up to £100,000 (I am trying to imagine what my bank would have to do to me that was worth even £1,000, but there you go.) They are independent and impartial and not the banks' poodles.

Direct Selling Association Limited
Website: www.dsa.org.uk

Members follow a code of practice which has been endorsed by the Director of Fair Trading. Apart from offering a unique 14-day cooling off period, the DSA's aim is to offer consumers 'a degree of consumer protection that is at least the equal of any of their competitors in other forms of retailing'.

Court Service (claim forms, etc)
Website: www.courtservice.gov.uk

And now – an A to Z of useful organisations

We have not test driven them: they come from the OFT website.

The Advertising Standards Authority
Brook House
2 Torrington Place
London WC1E 7HW
Tel: 020 7580 5555

The Architects Registration Board
8 Weymouth Street
London W1W 5BU
Tel: 020 7580 5861

The Assay Office
Goldsmiths' Hall
Gutter Lane
London EC2V 8AQ
Tel: 020 7606 8975

Association of British Insurers
51 Gresham Street
London EC2V 7HQ
Tel: 020 7600 3333

Association of British Travel Agents
68–71 Newman Street
London W1P 4AH
Tel: 0901 201 50 50 (50p/min)

Association of Master Upholsterers
Francis Vaughn House
102 Commercial Street
Newport
Gwent NP9 1LU
Tel: 01633 215454

Association of Independent Tour Operators
133a St Margarets Road
Twickenham
Middlesex TW1 1RG
Tel: 020 8744 9280

The Association of Manufacturers of Domestic Electrical Appliances
Rapier House
40–46 Lambs Conduit Street
London WC1N 3NW
Tel: 020 7405 0666

Air Travel Organiser's Licence (ATOL)
Civil Aviation Authority
45–59 Kingsway
London WC2B 6TE
Tel: 020 7832 5620/6600

Chartered Association of Certified Accountants
29 Lincolns Inn Fields
London WC2A 3EE
Tel: 020 7242 6855

Chartered Institute of Arbitrators
24 Angel Gate
City Road
London EC1V 2RS
Tel: 020 7837 4483

Architects Registration Council of The United Kingdom
73 Hallam Street
London W1N 6EE
Tel: 020 7580 5861

British Association of Removers
3 Churchill Court
58 Station Road
North Harrow
Middlesex HA2 7SA
Tel: 020 8861 3331

British Carpet Technical Centre – CAMRASO
Wira House
West Park Ring Road
Leeds LS16 6QL
Tel: 0113 259 1999

British Interior Textiles Association
Reedham House
31 King Street West
Manchester M3 2PF
Tel: 0161 832 8684

British Bathroom Council
Federation House
Station Road
Stoke-on-Trent
Staffs ST4 2RT
Tel: 01782 747074

British Decorators Association
32 Coton Road
Nuneaton
Warwickshire CV11 5TW
Tel: 01203 353776

British Holiday & Home Parks Association Ltd
Chichester House
6 Pullman Court
Great Western Road
Gloucester GL1 3ND
Tel: 01452 526911

British Association of Toy Retailers
24 Baldwyn Gardens
London W3 6HL
Tel: 020 8993 2894

British Retail Consortium
5 Grafton Street
London W1X 3LB
Tel: 020 7647 1500

British Institute of Professional Photography
Fox Talbot House
Amwell End
Ware
Herts SG12 9HN
Tel: 01920 464011

British Standards Institution
British Standards House
389 Chiswick High Road
London W4 4AL
Tel: 020 8996 9600; Fax: 0181 996 7400

Builder's Merchants Federation
15 Soho Square
London W1V 6HL
Tel: 020 7439 1753

The Charity Commission
St Alban's House
57-60 Haymarket
London SW1Y 4QX
Tel: 020 7210 4477

Commission for Racial Equality
Elliot House
10–12 Allington Street
London SW1E 5EH
Tel: 020 7828 7022

Companies House
Crown Way
Cardiff CF4 3UZ
Tel: 01222 388 588

Confederation of Roofing Contractors
72 Church Road
Brightlingsea
Colchester
Essex CO7 0JF
Tel: 01206 306600

Contract Flooring Association
4c St Mary's Place
off St Mary's Gate
The Lace Market
Nottingham NG1 1PH
Tel: 0115 941 1126

Council for Registered Gas Installers
4 Elmwood
Chineham Business Park
Crockford Lane
Basingstoke
Hants RG24 8WG
Tel: 01256 707060

The Customer Relations Adviser
Society of Motor Manufacturers and Traders
Forbes House
Halkin Street
London SW1X 7DS
Tel: 020 7235 7000

The Conciliation Service
The Vehicle Builders and Repairers Association
Belmont House
102 Finkle Lane
Gildersome
Leeds LS27 7TW
Tel: 0113 253 8333

The Data Protection Registrar
Wycliffe House
Water Lane
Wilmslow
Cheshire SK9 5AF
Tel: 01625 535 777

The Department of Trade and Industry
Consumer Affairs Division
10–18 Victoria Street
London SW1H 0NN
Tel: 020 7215 5000; Fax: 020 7222 9280

Direct Marketing Association
Haymarket House
1 Oxendon Street
London SW1Y 4EE

Domestic Appliance Service Association
71 The Maltings
Stanstead Abbots
Herts SG12 8MG
Tel: 01920 872464

Direct Selling Association
29 Floral Street
London WC2E 9DP
Tel: 020 7497 1234

Academy of Experts
2 South Square
Gray's Inn
London WC1R 5HP
Tel: 020 7637 0333

Fabric Care Research Association
Forest House Laboratories
Knaresborough Road
Harrogate HG2 7LZ
Tel: 01423 885977

Federation of Master Builders
Bush House
Bush Estate
Midlothian EH26 0SB
Tel: 0131 445 5577

Footwear Examination Centre
249 Rockingham Road
Kettering
Northamptonshire NN16 9JH
Tel: 01536 410000

Furniture Industry Research Association (FIRA International)
Maxwell Road
Stevenage
Herts SG1 2EW
Tel: 01438 313433

Glass and Glazing Federation
44-48 Borough High Street
London SE1 1XB
Tel: 020 7403 7177

Guild of Master Craftsmen
Castle Place
166 High Street
Lewes
East Sussex BN7 1XU
Tel: 01273 478 449

Heating and Ventilating Contractors' Association
ESCA House
34 Palace Court
London W2 4HY
Tel: 020 7229 2488

HPI-Equifax – The Used Car Information Line
PO Box 61
New Street
Dolphin House
Salisbury SP1 2TB
Tel: 01722 413434

ICSTIS
4th Floor
Clove Building
4 Maguire Street
London SE1 2NQ
Tel: 020 7940 7474

Independent Television Commission
33 Foley Street
London W1P 7LB
Tel: 020 7255 3000

League of Professional Craftsmen
10 Village Way
Rayners Lane
Pinner
Middlesex HA5 5AF
Tel: 020 8866 6116

Mail Order Trader's Association
40 Waterloo Road
Birkdale, Southport PR8 2NG
Tel: 01704 563787

Mail Order Protection Scheme (MOPS)
16 Tooks Court
London EC4A 1LB
Tel: 020 7405 6806

Mailing/Telephone Preference Service
FREEPOST 22
London W1E 7EZ
Tel: 0345 034599

National Weights and Measures Laboratory
Stanton Avenue
Teddington
Middlesex TW11 0JZ
Tel: 020 8943 7272; Fax: 020 8943 7270

National Consumers' Council
20 Grosvenor Gardens
London SW1W 0DH
Tel: 020 7730 3469

Electrical Contractors' Association
ESCA House
34 Palace Court
London W2 4HY
Tel: 020 7229 1266

Office of Fair Trading
Fleetbank House
2–6 Salisbury Square
London
EC4Y 8JX
Tel: 020 7242 2858; Fax: 020 7269 8800

Consumer Information Line
Tel: 0345 224499 (local call rates apply)
The Office of Fair Trading also has a series of free leaflets.
For an up-to-date list, write to:
Office of Fair Trading
PO Box 366
Hayes UB3 1XB
Tel: 0870 60 60 321
Fax. 0870 60 70 321
oft@echristian.co.uk
Publications can also be ordered from the OFT's website on the Internet

Optical Consumer Complaints Service
PO Box 4685
London SE1 6ZB
Tel: 020 7261 1017

Plastics Window Federation
Federation House
87 Wellington Street
Luton
Beds LU1 5AF
Tel: 01582 456147

Institute of Plumbing
64 Station Lane
Hornchurch
Essex RM12 6NB
Tel: 01708 472791

Chief Conciliation Officer
Qualitas National Conciliation Service
Maxwell Road
Stevenage
Herts SG1 2EW
Tel: 01438 316100

Retail Motor Industry Federation
2nd Floor, Chestnut House
9 North Street
Rugby CV21 2AB
Tel: 01788 538316

The Radio, Electrical and Television Retailer's Association Ltd
RETRA House
St. John's Terrace
1 Ampthill Street
Bedford MK42 9EY
Tel: 01234 269110

Royal Institute of Chartered Surveyors
12 Great George Street
Parliament Square
London SW1P 3AD
Tel: 020 7222 7000

Society of Master Shoe Repairers Ltd
St. Crispin's House
21 Station Road
Desborough
Northamptonshire NN14 2SA
Tel: 01536 760374

The Timeshare Council
23 Buckingham Gate
London SW1E 6LB
Tel: 020 7821 8845

Textile Services Association Ltd
7 Churchill Court
58 Station Road
North Harrow
Middlesex HA2 7SA

Ombudsmen

Commission for Local Administration in England
(Local Government Ombudsman)
21 Queen Anne's Gate
London SW1H 9BU
Tel: 020 7915 3210

Office of the Banking Ombudsman
70 Grays Inn Road
London WC1X 8NB
Tel: 020 7404 9944

Building Societies Ombudsman
Millbank Tower
Millbank
London SW1P 4XS
Tel: 020 7931 0044

Insurance Ombudsman
City Gate One
135 Park Street
London SE1 9EA
Tel: 020 7928 7600
Consumer hotline: 0845 600 6666

Investment Ombudsman
4th Floor
6 Frederick's Place
London EC2R 8BT
Tel: 020 7796 3065

Office of the Ombudsman for Estate Agents
Beckett House
4 Bridge Street
Salisbury
Wiltshire SP1 2LX
Tel: 01722 333306

Funeral Ombudsman
26–28 Bedford Row
London WC1R 4HE
Tel: 020 7430 1112

Legal Services Ombudsman
22 Oxford Court
Oxford Street
Manchester M2 3WQ
Tel: 0161 236 9532

Pensions Ombudsman
11 Belgrave Road
London SW1V 1RB
Tel: 020 7834 9144

Personal Investment Authority
Ombudsman Bureau
Hertsmere House
Hertsmere Road
London E14 4AB
Tel: 020 7216 0016

Index

Printed in the United Kingdom by The Stationery Office Ltd, London
TJ005334 C20 10/01 653505 19585